Esquire Drinks

Drinks

An OPINIONATED & IRREVERENT GUIDE to DRINKING

by David Wondrich

HEARST BOOKS
A DIVISION OF STERLING PUBLISHING CO., INC.
NEW YORK

Produced by Bill SMITH STUDIO
Editorial Director: Jacqueline A. Ball
Cover Design: Eric Hoffsten
Creative Director: Justine Price
Art Direction: Eric Hoffsten
Production Director: Maureen O'Connor
Production: James Liebman and Brad Spiegel

Library of Congress Cataloging-in-Publication Data
Wondrich, David.
Esquire drinks : an opinionated and irreverent guide to drinking/ by David Wondrich.
p. cm.
ISBN 1-58816-205-2
1. Cocktails. 2. Drinking customs. I. Esquire. II. Title.
TW951.W566 2002
641.8′74—dc21
          2001039865

10 9 8 7 6 5 4 3 2 1

Published by Hearst Books,
A Division of Sterling Publishing Co., Inc.
387 Park Avenue South, New York, N.Y. 10016

www.esquire.com

Distributed in Canada by Sterling Publishing
c/o Canadian Manda Group, One Atlantic Avenue, Suite 105
Toronto, Ontario, Canada M6K 3E7
Distributed in Australia by Capricorn Link (Australia) Pty. Ltd.
P.O. Box 704, Windsor, NSW 2756 Australia

Manufactured in China

ISBN 1-58816-205-2

ACKNOWLEDGMENTS

To make an *Esquire Drinks*, combine:

1 part inspiration (Karen Rush, Melissa Clark)

1 part opportunity (Joshua Mack, David Granger, Jacqueline Deval, Janis Donnaud)

1 part assistance (Nick Noyes, Sherwin Dunner, William Grimes, Jonathan Downey, Cary Berger, Ted Haigh, Rusty Greenland)

Edit vigorously (Brendan Vaughan, Jackie Ball, Laura Tennen), pour into elegant format (Eric Hoffsten), garnish with illustrations (Justine Price, Jemma Gura) and serve.

To all of you—and to everyone else who helped in ways that don't fit into neat little categories (Abigail Anderson, Justin Makler)—thanks for your good advice and apologies for the places where my rude and froward daemon has led me to ignore it.

This book is dedicated to everybody I've ever had a drink with.

—DAVID WONDRICH

CONTENTS

RULE #99

Ask yourself—
does the road
really need one?

INTRODUCTION

OKAY. **SO THIS ISN'T ABOUT DRINKING.** It's about drinking liquor. That's something all American grownups who didn't choose to opt out used to be able to do with a certain style, whether they took their firewater straight or mixed. Nowadays, many folks haven't got a clue. That at least is the conclusion we've been forced to after drinking our way through the barrooms and living rooms of modern America. Now, far be it for us to bust on our fellow citizens. But we wouldn't be *Esquire* if we didn't offer advice where it's needed.

It's needed. Case in point: a guy you know is having the boss and a couple of friends over for some tapas. Now, when it comes to beer and wine, the kind of person who's likely to buy an *Esquire* book—let's just say you could bet big money that he's not going to pass out individual cans of lite beer or crack open a jug of hearty California burgundy. But if you had to bet that he wasn't going to start the evening off with something dumb like bourbon and Kahlúa, or spiced rum and Gatorade, now that just might make you hedge….

It's not his fault. The last thirty-odd years have seen a whole tradition and mythology of drink relentlessly pushed aside by marketing-led 'innovation'—as in, "if you like that **Daiquiri*** with rum, you'll like it better with Professor McGuffin's™ Olde-Tyme Banana Schnapps"— and the same mindless drive for 'fun' and 'convenience' that has been recognized in virtually every other sector of American life as a cover for shoddy artificiality. As a result, most new drinks are syrupy swill fit only for the binge-drinking co-ed and the pledge who's trying to pin her.

* We've supplied recipes for all drinks printed in boldface; see the Drinks Index.

▲ **Cocktails are not for everyone. See Rule #548, opposite, while you're at it.**

Take the **Cum in a Hot Tub**. Two hundred years of cocktail history, and we're reduced to this. Splash a wad of Irish Cream into a shot glass of O.J., wait 'til it curdles and watch the co-eds suck 'em down by the hogshead. If it were called something innocuous—say, the Irish Orange—it's safe to say this train-wreck of mixology would be greeted with the scorn and revulsion it so richly deserves. But for youths whose hormone level is high enough to render their tastebuds paralyzed, the name is everything. To lecture your average undergrad shooter-Hoover on the use of quality ingredients and the finer points of mixing them is about as useful as making him—or her, God knows—sign a plagiarism pledge. In other words, you won't find shooters in here.

But surely there's more to contemporary mixology than the shooter. What about that whole **Martini** business? Sophisticated adults in nice clothes drinking things out of conical glasses on stems? It's true, the revival of the cocktail as an icon of urbane hedonism has conveyed numerous benefits on the discriminating drinker. Unfortunately, most of them are less spiritual than material, to be found largely in the realms of cool glassware and retro bar gadgets. The cocktails themselves, both the new and the new interpretations of the old classics, tend to be made weak, bland and oversweet.

We've done a little study. In the course of curating *Esquire*'s online Drinks Database, from which this book has sprung (visit www.esquire.com), we've encountered a great many new drinks, to which our *Esquire* Cocktail Contest (see the **Esquire**) has added a couple hundred more. Most of them fall into one or more of the following six categories:

1. **VODKA + X, OR CHILDREN OF THE SCREWDRIVER.** This is probably the largest class of new drinks. Take a fruit juice (bottled or fresh), a liqueur, a soft drink—anything, really—and smack it with a stick of beverage alcohol in its least-flavorful form. Simple and hard to screw up, but utterly predictable and depressingly un-American in its lack of ingenuity.

2. **BUG JUICE.** The type of drink that adulterates good booze (or not so good) with anything prepackaged, artificially-flavored, preservative-infused. Example: the tipple a reader sent in calling for citrus-flavored rum and "2 spoonfuls of Country Time Lemonade Mix." There's really nothing good to be said about these. Can you picture Humphrey Bogart ordering a vodka and Red Bull? Peppermint schnapps and 7-Up?

3. **THE MONOCHROME SET.** One dimension, repeated. Recent examples include the **Apple Martini**: vodka, sour-apple schnapps and muddled apple slices. And this thing, from a New York bar: mandarin-orange vodka with Cointreau (orange-flavored, you'll recall), Grand Marnier (likewise), orange juice, sour mix (not orange *per se*, but homeopathically related to the citrus family) and a tiny splash of Moët & Chandon champagne. After all that, it tastes like…orange. (Good thing they don't make orange Moët—yet.)

4. **LIQUEURAMA.** The other side of the coin: too much creativity. Kahlúa, amaretto and Frangelico in the same drink, or Cointreau, Midori (melon-flavored), crème de cacao (chocolate) and banana liqueur. Muddy in flavor, toothache-sweet and thick as Aunt Jemima syrup. Kiddie stuff.

5. **THE JUICE BOX.** Another shout out to childhood: three or more different fruit flavors, mixed with vodka or the lightest of rums, so all you can taste is a sweet, nonspecific fruitiness that brings to mind the flavor 'red.' The prime example is, of course, the **Cosmopolitan**, which combines the flavors of cranberry, lime and orange.

6. **KITCHEN ARTS.** American chefs have been coming up with some pretty kinky combinations of late—you know, ginger-jackfruit glazed breast of Muscovy duck on a bed of potato-quince purée with a reduction of so on and so forth. New kwizeen. This appears to have induced toque-envy in a goodly number of otherwise-decent bartenders. Result: champagne with sweetened, jellied elderflower puree, or rosemary-infused vodka with fresh tomato-water and a sprig of candied woodruff (that's an herb). Perhaps not bad drinks, per se, but we're naturally suspicious of any gloom-lifter that requires resources of a two-star restaurant kitchen to put it together. And again, the Bogart test applies.

RULE #548

If you can't taste the alcohol, you won't respect the drink; that way danger lies.

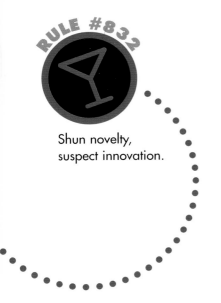

Now, not being total curmudgeons, we're willing to admit that it's not a lead-pipe cinch that a drink which fits into one of these classes will suck. Some things just taste good. In fact, you can find at least one true classic cocktail for each class. Bug Juice? **Cuba Libre**. Kitchen Arts? **Pisco Punch**. We've even managed to make a kind of peace with the **Cosmopolitan**. But let's be realistic. When the money is on the bar, a combo like white rum and Diet Squirt (really!) will never, ever measure up to even so plain an old stand-by as the **Gin Rickey**. Besides, do you really want to *order* that?

The real problem? Drinks like these, they're just not…well, *manly*. Can we say that? Probably not. *Honest*, then. There's something a little shameful about them. A square drink should enhance the taste of the liquor in it; these disguise it. Rather than do what they're doing without cuteness, evasion or apology, they weasel. It's a matter of conviction: you're either the kind of person who drinks something that says "you really can't taste the liquor," or the kind who drinks something that says "hell yes, that's liquor—wanna make something of it?" When you're drinking a **Martini**, a real one, you know you're drinking gin.

But instead of continuing to foam at the mouth about the current state of affairs, we've decided to go back to the basics; to drink our way through the old classics and try to figure out just what it was that made 'em that way. What separates a **Sidecar** from a Sex on the Beach? It's not just the name. The Age of the Cocktail, when mixology was in its full fighting trim, ran from about 1870, when the **Martini** was invented, to 1960, when people started drinking them on the rocks. The art had its ups and downs—folks drank frightful things during Prohibition—but throughout, there was general agreement on the basic philosophical principles of the art. A true cocktail should take the pronounced, even pungent, flavor of a liquor and, through careful blending with aromatics, acids and essences, transform it, without erasing it, into something smooth and bracing and unlike anything else. And if this isn't as easy as mixing Jack Daniels and Dr. Pepper, it's not exactly mapping the human genome, either. A little patience, a little extra effort, and suddenly you're drinking like a grownup.

In that spirit, we present this, *Esquire*'s seventh drinks book. (We've been doing 'em since 1939, when we put out a little ring-bound *Liquor Intelligencer*.) Within, you'll find some 244 time-tested ways to get the best out of your firewater. And if there are no mixtures of fruited-up vodkas with energy drinks, neither will you find a bunch of old relics that nobody would possibly make—no Blue Blazers and Bunny Hugs, no Cobblers, Flips and Sangarees (well, one or two, maybe). We've looked for drinks that will work in 2002 as well as they did in 1902 or 1952. Drinks you can make, and make right even when you've had a couple. (With the occasional necessary exception—see the **Ramos Fizz**—we've kept exotic ingredients and complex procedures to a minimum.) But that's only part of the story. There are lots of books that'll tell you how to make a given drink. *Esquire Drinks* is also going to try to convince you why.

Consider, on the one hand, 5 cl of C_2H_5OH—alcohol—administered orally in a semifrigid aqueous solution. On the other, a bone-dry **Vodka Martini**. Chemically, the exact same thing. But in the real world we live in, as different as Madonna and The Madonna. Drinks (the best of them, anyway) are more than just the sum of their ingredients. Each recognized formula, if it's been around for a while, has had to make room for the lingering presence of all the people, places and events with which it's been associated. This isn't the same as a history, precisely; there's too much rumor and lore associated with drinks for that. Call it a myth. And, like all myths, those that congregate around drinks are slippery things. We've done our best to pin 'em down, but if we've let one or another wiggle away, be a sport and round it up for us? You know where to find us—at least, between the hours of five and seven.

And so, Ladies and Gents, what'll it be?

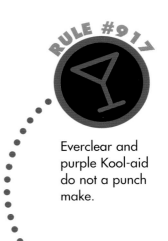

RULE #917

Everclear and purple Kool-aid do not a punch make.

PART I:

Alcohol

...AND HOW TO MIX IT

(top) High-tech medievalism: state-of-the-art pot stills at Scotland's Glen Moray distillery.

A FREEWHEELING HISTORY OF HOOCH

ALCOHOL AND CIVILIZATION GO HAND IN HAND. Whenever archaeologists dig out another one of those unimaginably old ruins of mud-walled villages, they always turn up the traces of some kind of tipple, some primitive fermentate of honey, or barley, or grapes—or even a combination of them (mixology is truly an ancient art).

The Egyptians, the Greeks, the Romans, the Chinese all had surprisingly modern beverage industries, complete with expensive imports and wine snobs. What they didn't have, however, is hooch. Distilled spirit.

That's as far as we can tell, anyway. History on alcohol is, like anyone on alcohol, sentimental, credulous, loose with the facts and plagued by frequent blackouts. The who, what, where, when, even the why of the invention of distilled spirits are shrouded in gloom. Sure, legends abound—the Chinese made hooch in the first millennium B.C., Aristotle knew about it, St. Patrick made whiskey in the 600s, it's an ancient Indian art. The most common story credits it to the Arabs. This one seems pretty solid, what with 'alcohol' being derived, somehow, from the Arabic word *kohl*, or powdered antimony (that stuff belly dancers use to rim their eyes). Unfortunately, it's bullshit.

According to R. J. Forbes's *Short History of the Art of Distillation*, the most recent scholarly history of the topic, there are few, if any, verifiable traces of the production of spirits before the Middle Ages, and certainly nothing on a significant scale. We're not saying it didn't happen, just that all those stories about when and where have a distressing tendency to vanish in a puff of smoke when you poke them. On the other hand, 'most recent' in this case means 1949, liquor studies being nowhere as popular these days within the ivory tower as, e.g., culture studies—if only drunks were as organized as post-structuralists.

'Proof' was originally defined as a liquor that was 50 percent alcohol; 86 proof, therefore, would be 86 percent of that.

At any rate, there's pretty good evidence that the standard pot still—the old bulb-topped container with a pipe sticking out of its head—was thought up by the Egyptian alchemist known as Maria the Jewess, around the first or second century A.D., or by one of her buddies. Yet, incredibly, she and her fellow-mystics found better things to do with this revolutionary equipment than making booze (what's gold got that liquor hasn't?). Weird, but not as weird as it seems.

Here's the problem. Distillation is easy. Alcohol vaporizes at 173° F (78.5° C), water at 212° (100°); theoretically, all you have to do is boil up something with a little alcohol in it (just leave any sweet liquid uncovered for a few days), collect the early part of the steam, condense it, and there's your hooch. It's potent, portable and non-perishable. The hard part is making it potable.

There are a couple of wrinkles in the process that make this tricky. To begin with, a fair amount of the water in your wash (the term of art for whatever it is you're trying to distill) will vaporize early and a fair amount of the alcohol will vaporize late. So the first pass through a pot still yields what those in the biz call 'low wines', which—as the name implies—aren't exactly firewater. At about 20 to 25 percent alcohol, they're only twice as potent as a good, strong red wine, and nowhere near as tasty. Furthermore, the wash always has a few extra compounds in it besides alcohol and water. Some of these—fusel oils and such—are rather toxic. If you don't know what you're doing, they'll end up in the low wines, guaranteeing the hangover of death.

Of course, you can purify the low wines by running them through the still again. Some of the impurities will come out, and proof will go up (to a practical maximum of about 75 to 80 percent), but these 'high wines' have little in common with liquor as you know it—unless you're accustomed to buying your stuff in gallon milk jugs from a guy named Earl. It takes real finesse to turn this liquid nitro into something you'd drink by choice. And that finesse, as in so many things, seems to have come from the Italians.

Italy, in the high Middle Ages—roughly, the 1100s through the 1300s—was the fairest part of Christendom: more or less peaceful, learned in the arts and sciences, relatively well-governed and, most importantly, rich. Whether or not others had been toying with distilling wine into alcohol before that, it was then that the Italians began turning it into an industry. Starting in the 1100s, references to *aqua vitae* ('water of life') and *aqua ardens* ('burning water') begin turning up in cutting-edge Italian alchemical manuals and advanced (no sniggering, please) medical treatises. By the beginning of the 1200s, brainy types from one end of the boot to the other are fiddling with the new technology, streamlining it and making the usual improvements. Are they the first to separate out the so-called 'heads', (the fusel oils and other light compounds that vaporize even before the alcohol) and the heavier 'tails' (mostly water and other organic muck) from the heart—the good stuff? We don't know. We do know that it's an Italian who, toward the end of the thirteenth century, solves the cooling problem that had been keeping the pot still from achieving its full potential by bending the outflow-pipe of his still into the familiar serpentine curves and immersing it in cool, running water. Thaddaeus Florentinus, we salute you.

But before we go any farther with what comes out of the still, let's talk for a minute about what goes into it. Spirits have been made in every country in the world, under all circumstances, from everything that has any kind of sugar in it whatsoever, or anything—starches, mostly—that can be turned into sugar: sugarcane itself, naturally, and fruits and grains of all species. But also the sap of the Asian date palm and the American sugar maple. And mare's milk and coconut milk. And potatoes, beets and other roots, including those of the Hawaiian *ti* plant (whose leaves give us the grass skirt) and the Brazilian tapioca. And cactus juice and cashew nuts and even Indian butter-tree flowers (which, according to one authority, have "an unfortunate and disgusting smell of mice"). If you haven't got anything else, leftovers will do—potato peels, the stems and skins left over from pressing wine, the residue from sugar-refining, like that. Folks have even made hooch out of rotten grain, spoiled wine and plain old wood. Not good hooch, but hooch nonetheless. Yet out of all this plenty—a true testament to the power of thirst as a motor for human ingenuity—only a handful of raw materials have proven themselves suitably cheap and versatile to produce anything more than a local curiosity.

Fruit juices are the easiest to work with: their sugar content is high, they supply their own liquid, and they ferment naturally. Most, however, are too

Alchemical laboratory, vintage 1948: San Francisco's legendary Vesuvio Café. ▼

strongly flavored to produce the kind of workhorse spirit that's good for day-in, day-out tippling. Fruit liquors, or *eaux-de-vie*, as they're known (*eau de vie* is French for our old pal *aqua vitae*), are popular in the wilder parts of Europe, and strictly niche items everywhere else—how many shots of apricot brandy do you really want to put down? One, a delicious novelty. Two, still not bad. Three, enough with the apricots, already.

There is, of course, one exception. As far as fruits go, grapes don't have a hell of a lot of flavor. Paradoxically, that's a good thing, at least when it comes to long-haul tippling. For one thing, it means that the resulting spirit—brandy, from the Dutch for 'burnt wine' (the Dutch were, and are, demon distillers)—can be used as a medium for other flavors; most French and Italian liqueurs are based on grape spirits, along with such tipples as the anise-flavored 'arak' of the Middle East. For another, it means that there's nothing to overpower the subtle flavors the stuff takes on with age—but we'll get to that in a moment.

Grapes don't grow well in cold climates or tropical ones. Luckily, the peoples of Northern Europe had an alternative close at hand: malt. When grains begin to sprout, certain enzymes convert the starches in them into sugars—and we know what you can do with sugars. Malting the grain, as this process is called, adds a few more steps to the process of distilling, but what's a little labor when you get a nice, neutral firewater out of it? (Besides, if it's barley you're malting, the enzymes are so potent they'll convert the starches in all the grains you mix with it, as well. This can save time and money.) By the 1400s, the Scots, the Irish, the English and the Dutch were distilling barley, while the Germans, the Poles and the Russians—and the Ukrainians, Letts, Kashubians and other proud peoples of the north—were distilling wheat and, especially, rye.

The other side of the climactic coin was taken care of sometime after 1493, when sugarcane arrived in the New World, and somebody in the Caribbean started distilling its juice (which, it turned out, was so rich that you could even process out much of the sugar and distill the molasses that was left behind). Between grape, grain and cane, you've got the raw materials for most of the myriad liquors and liqueurs made in the world today.

So Noah when he anchor'd safe on The Mountain's top, his lofty haven, He made it next his chief design To plant and to propagate a vine, Which since has overwhelm'd and drown'd Far greater numbers, on dry ground, Of wretched mankind, one by one, Than all the flood before had done.

—SAMUEL BUTLER,
"A SATIRE ON DRUNKENNESS"

Okay, so you've run your wash, whatever it is, through the ol' pot-and-coil a couple of times and collected your jug of firewater. Now what? Three-fourths of what's in the jug is alcohol, pure and simple. Alcohol tastes like alcohol, no matter what you make it out of. It's how you handle the other fourth that determines how your tipple is going to turn out. That fourth, a mixture of water and various organic compounds (esters, aldehydes, phenolics and such, generally lumped together under the name 'congeners'), is both a problem and an opportunity—it's where the flavor is, but a lot of that flavor is harsh and nasty. (Some washes, we should point out, offer more problems and opportunities than others, depending on the raw material itself, the kind of yeast you use, and how long you let it ferment).

First, as just about everybody agrees, you've got to step on your product a little, bring the alcohol down to somewhere between 40 and 60 percent of the total. 'Proof' was originally defined as a liquor that was 50 percent alcohol, and that was the standard strength liquor was sold at, give or take a few degrees, until fairly recently. Nowadays, we tend to prefer something a little under that—most liquors are sold at 80 to 86 proof (that is, 80 to 86 percent of that original proof). But while dilution is necessary (have you tried doing shots of 151-proof rum? not pleasant), it won't make for good liquor all by itself. You've still got to do something about those congeners.

Logically, there are three approaches to the problem: add things, subtract things, change what's there. All have been tried—when it comes to drink, humans are persistent little critters. The easiest way is to mask the congeners, good and bad, with some other flavor. The Italians, first with the still, seem to have been first to figure out how to make the raw spirit go down easy by sweetening the hell out of it and flavoring it with herbs, spices, fruits, nuts—whatever. The resulting liqueurs—what we're looking at here—were marketed as medicines. Of course, it wasn't long before they were being taken, let's say, preventively. Everybody deserves a little pick-me-up now and then, right? If you've ever enjoyed a Frangelico or a Fernet Branca, a Chartreuse or a Bénédictine (in 1332, the Italians brought liqueur-making to France), you can see the appeal.

Oh corn-ricks and rye-ricks,
Oh corn-ricks are bonnie...
—SCOTTISH FOLKSONG

The only way you'll impress people by using that 30-year-old cognac (or Scotch, or…) to mix drinks with is as an idiot.

But all that sugar can cloy. Sooner or later, folks started leaving it out. The best surviving example of the resulting tipple is Dutch or Genever gin, invented in 1650 (the story goes) when one Doctor Franciscus Sylvius of the University of Leyden hit on the idea of adding juniper berries and a raft of other, similarly pungent herbs and spices to the grain mash from which the Dutch distilled their customary care-killer. (He also discovered the tubercules that give tuberculosis its name and founded the first university chem lab; curse or cheer as you prefer). Dr. Sylvius's tipple is dry but full-bodied, with a roiling undertaste of the grain from which it's distilled. London dry gin (the technical name for what we know as plain old gin), is a whole different animal. It uses more or less the same flavorings, sure. But the raw spirit upon which it's based has had most of its flavor, good and bad, ruthlessly stripped away.

There are two ways to cleanse your hooch of congeners: filter them out, or distill them out. The great filtration specialists were the Russians and the Poles. By the mid-eighteenth century, after years of running their pot-stilled korchma (the term *vodka*, 'little water', doesn't seem to have come in before the nineteenth century) through everything from felt to sand, they hit on the idea of trying charcoal. This worked, yielding a clean-tasting, light spirit—especially if you used beechwood (although birch is almost as good, and much cheaper).

The pot still, however, is a pretty inefficient way of separating spirit from body. Even after filtering, pot-stilled vodka retains some vestiges of body and flavor. What's more, it's strictly a single-shot, muzzle-loading kind of device. Not only do you have to run it twice, but after every run, you've got to let it cool and then clean it out. And even then, it's tough getting a really pure spirit out of it. If you're using good materials—decent wine, malted barley, fresh cider—that's not so much of a problem. But what if, from greed or necessity, you're using crap? The alcohol will taste the same, regardless. Can't you just get rid of everything else entirely? Then it wouldn't matter a bit if your wash was made from pig-slops.

The nineteenth century, an age that thought a good deal about progress and perfectability, not at all about unintended consequences, took up the problem of the pot still and its quaint old defects with characteristic headlong vigor. The solution, patented by the Frenchman Jean-Baptiste Cellier Blumenthal in 1818, was the distilling column: a tall, heated copper cylinder with a bunch of perforated plates inside. You run your wash in at the middle and, as it drips down from plate to plate, the steam from the residue bubbling away at the bottom of the column rises through the plates, in part condensing and dripping back down, but also in part vaporizing the lighter parts of the wash—congeners, some water and, of course, alcohol. As this vapor rises further, it condenses on the plates above, the lightest parts last. Figure out which plate the alcohol ends up at, and there's your tap—final product: 85 to 95 percent pure. (Got all that?)

Unlike the pot still, you could run one of these babies continuously, pumping out the spent wash as you pumped in the fresh. And it used less fuel. And you didn't need a lot of cold, running water for the condenser. In other words, cheap hooch. The first users of the so-called 'patent still' came from the shadowy world of industrial alcohol, who turned it loose on beet juice and suchlike. In 1830, though, Aeneas Coffey, an Irishman working in Scotland, patented his version of the continuous still, using two columns (one to heat the stuff up and one to cool it down) to make whiskey, of a sort, from grain.

Most liquors today are made with some version of the column still. That doesn't mean they're all flavorless: if you play the column right, you can draw off some of the congeners with your alcohol, although this takes skill and effort—money, in other words. But as a rule, a column-stilled product will be lighter in body and cleaner in taste (and much cheaper to make) than a pot-stilled one. For many uses, you want this: it provides a nice, white-paint background for liqueurs and flavored liquors such as our London dry gin, aquavit (flavored with caraway seeds, of all things) and schnapps, and it gives vodka and, to a lesser extent, white rum and tequila their raison d'être. Often you'll find column-distilling combined with charcoal filtering, for a suspenders-and-a-belt approach to purity that makes it very hard indeed to tell what it was that went into the still. Hell, you can get good vodka out of potatoes.

Some liquors, however, *like* flavor, which brings us to our final approach. Transformation. What if you could change the wicked congeners into good ones? Alchemy, in other words: lead into gold. There is, it turns out, a simple way to do this. It seems to have been discovered quite by accident. Back in the Renaissance, y'see, western France had a pretty lively sea trade going, shipping wine up north to the parts of the continent where thirsts were hearty and wine scarce. The rest of Europe liked to store its wine in whale-sized casks, where it aged without much interaction with the wood. But loading those onto the little wooden ships France used to trade with its neighbors? Nightmare. Around Bordeaux, the folks took to putting their wine in 50 to 60 gallon barrels, made from the local oak (with results too well-known to need going into). When the merchants of the Charente, the coastal region north of Bordeaux centered around the small town of Cognac, started boiling their wine into brandy (they had to: straight, it wasn't good), it was only natural for them to borrow a page from their neighbors' playbook.

Nowadays, we know all about what happens when you do that, and keep it there for a long time and all about how a percentage of the new brandy escapes each year through the pores of the wood (*la part des anges*, as they call it—'the angels' share') and how the congeners interact with both the air that takes its place and the compounds that leach out of the oak (lignins and tannins and even sugars, produced from the starches in the wood when the barrel-maker toasts it to make it bendable), until what went into the keg tasting like home-refined kerosene comes out a nectar to surpass Keats's blushful Hippocrene. (John Keats, by the way, wasn't much of a drinker—"I never drink above three glasses of wine," he wrote to a friend, "and never any spirits and water." Why are we not surprised?)

Then, it wasn't so obvious. While aging in oak starts to work its wonders after only a year or so, and makes definite improvements after four, it takes eight to twelve years for real mellowness to set in, and double that for the liquor's true inner beauty to emerge. And who the hell would let inventory sit around that long out of mere curiosity? Eventually, they figured it out. Whether that first happened in the early 1600s, in the Charente, as certain interested parties claim, we don't know. We do know that, by the eighteenth century, the aged brandies of the Charente had achieved a worldwide renown which they've maintained through thick and thin ever since. (The letters on the bottle? VS: 'Very Superior', which means at least two and a half years in oak; VSOP: 'Very Superior Old Pale', four and a half years; XO: 'Extra Old', six years; these are minimums, and a good XO may have slept in the barrel for as long as forty years.)

In due time, barrel aging spread to Scotland and Ireland and even America. Before that, whiskey was nothing like the golden elixir we know today. It was a white grain spirit, strong and pungent. Think white lightnin'. Think thick, spicy vodka; in Scotland, what's more, it was traditional to dry the malt in peat smoke, giving it an extra smoky tang which it still retains. ('Whiskey', by the way, comes from the Gaelic *uisge beatha* (Scots) or *usquebaugh* (Irish), 'water of life'—*aqua vitae*, in other words, which gives you a pretty good idea where the Celtic peoples of the British Isles were looking when they invented the stuff.) Now, even tequila—once the most low-down of spirits—rests for a good while in wood, with salutary results.

The combination of pot stilling and barrel aging is the hard way of making liquor, but if you like layer upon layer of deep, rich flavor, it's the way to go. Cognac and single-malt Scotch—the two kinds of liquor with the most, we dunno, class, cachet, whatever—use the pot and barrel. To them you can add a few so-called 'liqueur' rums, even a couple of American whiskies. All expensive to make and, naturally, expensive to buy.

Luckily, barrel-aging adds depth and mellowness to column-stilled spirits, too. Few bourbons bother with pot stills, and yet give 'em a few years in wood and they're in there swinging with the best of 'em. You can also blend the wood-aged stuff (however it was distilled) with white spirit straight out of the still, using the aged to flavor the raw, the raw to stretch out the aged. Hence blended Scotch, which is often very good, and blended (American) whiskey, which seldom is. Many rums are blends as well, but those have to be explored on a case-by-case basis (nothing in the wide world of hooch is more complicated than rum).

Just about every one of the three main raw materials has been tried, somewhere, with every congener-tamer, both singly and in combination. There are so many variables involved (we've barely skimmed the surface) that one little change can make a world of difference. Grain—column still—filtering—barrel aging? Jack Daniel's. Cane—column still—barrel aging—filtering? Bacardi Carta Blanca (the white stuff—lots of filtering). Distilling hooch is one case where tinkering pays off.

Whisky or whiskey? In Scotland and Canada, it's always "ky"; in KY (and the rest of the States) and Ireland, it's usually "key." (Benrinnes, by the way, is in Scotland.) ▼

AMERICA DRINKS (IN BRIEF)

J **UST ABOUT EVERY LIQUOR EVER MADE** has been popular in America at some point (well, not the butter-tree stuff). Nonetheless, liquor drinking in America falls into four ages.

THE RUM AGE

Rum was the heart-blood of the New World. Whoever started distilling cane juice in its various forms, wherever that was, by the mid-1600s everybody in the Caribbean was making rum (nobody's sure where the name comes from; theories abound). They needed it, you see. As Richard Ligon explained in his 1657 *True and Exact Account of the Island of Barbadoes*, "certainly strong drinks are very requisite, where so much heat is…the spirits being exhausted with much sweating, the inner parts are left cold and faint, and shall need comforting and reviving." That's a fact.

But you also needed it in cold climates, it turned out, and in temperate ones, too. In 1700, the first rum distillery in North America was built in Boston. By 1763, there were 159 of them in New England alone, all using Caribbean molasses. It took this domestic product—the British colonies' first industrial success and soon their largest industry—no time at all to spread to the farthest, most inaccessible corners of the new land. In 1728, Colonel William Byrd of Virginia was traveling through the wilds of North Carolina, where he found no shortage of the stuff—they even fried bacon in it and drank the drippings, which "serv'd…at once for meat and Drink." Byrd observed, "Most of the rum they get in this Country comes from New England and is so bad and unwholesome, that it is not improperly call'd 'Kill-Devil.'" No matter. Folks drank it anyway, morning, noon and night, in staggering quantities—along with beer, hard cider, imported wines, cherry brandy, peach brandy, applejack (distilled hard cider, a specialty of New Jersey), etc., etc. Americans, it turned out, were different from Europeans chiefly in the fact that they liked liquor more than just about anyone else on the planet. This bit of authentic Early American doggerel about covers it:

> There's but one Reason I can think
> Why People ever cease to drink:
> Sobriety the Cause is not,
> Nor Fear of being deem'd a Sot:
> But if Liquor can't be got.

That was seldom to be a problem.

The American Revolution put a hefty dent in the rum trade, what with the English shutting off the unending stream of molasses that had been flowing into the colonies. Rum maintained its niche, though: as late as the winter of 1871, a survey in the *New York World* of a day's trade at thirteen saloons "in the vicinity of Wall Street, patronized principally by the brokers," found that, of the 4,016 drinks of liquor dispensed, 713 were hot spiced rums. On the other hand, the brokers sank 1223 straight whiskeys and 830 hot ones.

THE WHISKEY AGE

When it came to strong drink, in America the nineteenth century was all about whiskey. Whiskey was the drink of Manifest Destiny, the fuel that propelled a grasping and irrepressible people across a continent. That whiskey, though, wasn't bourbon, nowadays synonymous with American whiskey. It was rye. America's first (and, as far as we're concerned, best) indigenous liquor. Straight rye is to bourbon as Scotch is to Irish: funkier, sharper, less generous and more intense.

Some history. In the 1600s, the English had planted a large number of Presbyterian—Protestant—Scots in the midst of Catholic Ireland. By the early 1700s, many of these Ulstermen left for America, spurred on by ruinous rents and various agricultural disasters. They liked it here: between 1717 and 1776, at least a quarter million of them came over. What's more, in the middle of the century, the Ulstermen were joined by a goodly number of Scottish refugees from the English 'pacification' of the Highlands. The Scotch-Irish and especially the Highlanders were born bootleggers (been doing it for generations—the English had peculiar ideas about taxing liquor).

Many—most—of these new arrivals settled in Pennsylvania, where the government was liberal and the land was plentiful and the people drank rum. Rum was cheap, if you lived near transportation by the coast, and tasty, once you got used to it. Fortunately for the history of American whiskey, the Scotch-Irish didn't have much of a chance to learn about rum: the Colony's government took one look at them and shipped them out west. There, they found a hilly, well-timbered land with good soil and plenty of obscure little streams and not much government supervision. Exactly. Bootlegging, just like back home. The only problem: their traditional barley didn't do well over here. They found the solution among some of their neighbors—Germans, as it happened. There were a lot of them around, mostly pretty religious and not much interested in distilling, but some the opposite. Like back home, they made their *Schnaps* from rye, which turned out to grow pretty well over here. So the Celts learned how to malt rye (not so easy, but—thank God—doable).

By 1790, the biggest industry in western Pennsylvania was making 'Monongohela rye'—in the four counties around Pittsburgh, there were 570 known distilleries turning out 'good old Nongela', as it was known among the frontiersmen who drank it like water. In 1797, even George Washington, by then an ex-president with time on his hands, got into the act. James Anderson, his farm manager, was a Scot who knew the biz, and there was plenty of spare grain at Mount Vernon. When Washington did something, he did it right: by the time he went to his reward a couple of years later, he was turning out 11,000 gallons of rye a year—one of the biggest distillers in the country. First in the hearts of his countrymen indeed.

Meanwhile, partly to escape the new United States whiskey tax (some things never change), those same Celtic Americans were pushing themselves past the bounds of civilization, or at least Pennsylvania. West Virginia, western North Carolina, Kentucky, Tennessee. Places so far from transportation that it cost far more to get your surplus grain to market than the stuff was worth. There was no choice but to make whiskey. Honest. Out there on the frontier, folks like the Reverend Elijah Craig, Jacob Beam, Elijah Pepper and Basil Hayden were also discovering how easy corn was to grow, and how when you mixed a bunch of it in with your rye, the whiskey came out tasting just fine, if a little on the light side (think corn bread vs. rye bread). The center for this newfangled corn-liquor was Bourbon County, Kentucky.

Bourbon corn and Monongohela rye (or Maryland rye, for that matter—Maryland was big in the rye business) were white liquors, at first. Sure, they put it in barrels, but Americans were an exceptionally thirsty and impatient lot, and the odds of them leaving good hooch lying around for eight or ten years were pretty slim. The American way, though, is both/and, not either/or, and soon enough a way was discovered whereby you could age and smooth out your pop-skull in just three or four years. All you had to do was burn the inside of the barrel. Char it. Not only does the charcoal act as a kind of filter for some of the impurities in the whiskey, but the heat caramelizes some of the sugars in the wood, thus sweetening up your liquor and turning it a most attractive coppery red, to boot.

Nobody was there with a pen and paper when they figured this out, sometime before 1840. Probably an accident, though: the best way to clean out old barrels that had been used to store something funky—think salted fish—was to burn them out. It was worth it. Barrels weren't cheap. History does record that it was Dr. James Crow, a Kentuckian by way of Scotland, who—also around 1840—began experimenting with reserving a portion of his fermented corn mash and adding it to the next batch in place of yeast. When you do the same thing with bread dough, it's a 'sour' dough, so this, of course, is a sour mash. With charred-oak barrels and sour mash, the development of American whiskey was pretty much done. The rest of the century witnessed a ceaseless struggle between honest distillers and cheap fakers, men who'd doctor up raw grain alcohol with stuff like ether (!) and pass it off as good rye or bourbon.

The Bottled-in-Bond act of 1897 pretty much fixed shenanigans like those: store your whiskey in a government-bonded warehouse for four years, bottle it at a government-tested 100 proof, and get a government stamp of approval for the bottle. In 1907, further legislation required that blended whiskeys (straight whiskey plus grain alcohol) had to be labeled as such. Still more regulations would come in 1934, after Prohibition had been repealed: rye and bourbon had to be distilled at no more than 160 proof and aged at least two years in new, charred-oak barrels, and the mashbill had to be at least 51 percent rye for, well, rye, and 51 percent corn for bourbon. The other 49 percent? Rye generally uses some corn for smoothness, bourbon some rye for flavor—except when it uses wheat for extra lightness of body. Both bourbon and rye usually throw in a little barley malt, which has enzymes that aid fermentation.

Anyway, for a while, things in America were good, whiskey-wise. The Sons (and Daughters) of Dixie drank their bourbon and everyone else pretty much drank rye, which was the default whiskey. When, for example, an old cocktail recipe calls for 'whiskey', it's got rye in mind. The **Manhattan** was a rye drink, and still should be, we say. Then, in 1919, came Prohibition and the Volstead Act that enforced it. And gin.

THE GIN AGE

Gin made it over here early on: the Dutch set up a distillery on Staten Island in 1640, and we're willing to bet they tried their hands at the trendy new tipple that was knocking 'em dead back home. But then the Brits came, and—on this side of the pond, anyway—they preferred other things (back home, gin was fast establishing itself as the liquid precursor of crack—cheap, potent and deadly). Gin just didn't have much of a constituency here. But it didn't go away, either. Its peculiar bite and hot-rails-to-hell reputation won it converts among gamblers, frontiersmen and other folks who cut life close to the edge.

It took the **Martini**—a drink whose sublimity seems to have been recognized almost immediately, although its precise origins remain frustratingly obscure—to put gin over the top. Whenever it was first concocted, whoever first concocted it, by 1900 the **Martini** was one of the main markers of the dividing line between the old, rural America of farmers and other whiskey drinkers and the new, urban world of electricity and motor-cars, elevators and office-workers. As Bernard DeVoto, the curmudgeonly historian, put it, "The Martini is a city dweller, a metropolitan…. All cultural subtleties belong to the city." (See "The Hour," it's good stuff.)

The farmers didn't care for that kind of palaver, nor for the lurid city doings they were seeing in the illustrated press. They threw their lot in with the Prohibitionists. Ironically, this just meant that, when their thirst glands shook off their righteous paralysis, they had to drink gin like everybody else. Or, we should say, 'gin'—raw, home-distilled alcohol with essence of juniper (or 'juniper') sloshed into it to mask the taste. Far easier to make at home, or wherever, than good rye or bourbon. Everybody drank it.

Gin came roaring out of Prohibition with a momentum that carried it clear through the 1960s, leaving in its wake a trail of fewer and fewer vermouth bottles every year. The dry **Martini**—do we really have to get into that? If you don't know the cultural history of the **Martini** in the mid-twentieth century, rent *The Thin Man*. Just about any novel, any movie from 1933 to 1963, Westerns excepted, will have somebody ordering one, mixing one—complete with bartending tips—drinking one. But by the end of the Martini Age, things

had gotten all silly: there was all that my Martini's-dryer-than-your-Martini business, people doing anything to avoid adding any actual vermouth to their drink—leaving a capful of vermouth out to evaporate in the living room, letting the sun shine through the vermouth bottle onto the shaker, saluting in the direction of France.

As happens whenever folks get piggy with something, the backlash set in. Throughout the 1960s and 1970s, while happily dosing themselves with substances even more strangely intoxicating, the younger folks treated gin as if it were compounded from equal parts nuclear waste and Geritol. Meanwhile, vodka was quietly Pac-Manning up what remained of its market. Not even the greedy 1980s helped much. Martinis were drunk, sure, but they were **Vodka Martinis**. Yet gin still hangs on, sometimes in surprising places (see the **Orange Blossom**). Like powdered cocaine, it's got its cadre of hard-core addicts for whom no other intoxicant will do.

THE VODKA AGE

To talk about vodka, we've got to talk about its cousin in the grain, whiskey. While everybody was busy focusing on gin, a funny thing started happening on the whiskey front. As our Lawton Mackall put it in the August, 1940 *Esquire*, the "damn-Yankees" were "horning in on" bourbon and leaving rye behind (up to then, they'd been pretty much neck-and-neck). "Even in myopic New York City," he wrote, "I am informed the bourbon curve is climbing by leaps and bottles." Now, rye whiskey's a big, brawling, in-your-face kind of drink. It was whiskey with hair on its chest. That had been what people liked about it, but now it wasn't quite so cool anymore. Bourbon, while far from being a drink for cowards and milquetoasts, had a certain natural gentility that rye had to struggle to attain. Worse, bourbon and rye both were also feeling the heat from the hitherto-scorned blended whiskey, which got away with stretching out one part of the good stuff with from two to four parts neutral spirits. And there was Scotch, which came in during Prohibition and refused to leave. Seeing as this was the lighter blended stuff, not the more hardcore single-malt (that didn't really take off until the 1980s), this too can be seen as a symptom of decline.

Right then, with this crucial question in American tippling—is it gonna be the easy way or the rugged way, the comfort drink or the acquired taste?—still undecided, the War started. The answer was postponed. Suddenly, Uncle Sam found himself in need of truly gargantuan amounts of alcohol—and not because soldiers like a nip now and then. Alcohol, as it turns out, has all kinds of other uses, among them the manufacture of rubber and certain explosives (is there anything alcohol can't do?). So just about all the whiskey that used to go into new charred-oak barrels to sit for a spell went into tank tracks, torpedoes and 2,000-pound bombs instead. Fair enough.

When our boys were demobbed after the Allied victory, back in civvies and harboring something of a thirst, there was kind of a problem. The distilleries had lots of raw whiskey on hand, but they didn't have a hell of a lot of the aged stuff. So: blend 'em. And if the result doesn't have a lot of body or flavor, it's better than jungle juice, anyway, and it sure did go down easy.

Inevitably, Grimes's Law kicked in. You know, "bad hooch will drive out good, as long as it's easier to drink" (paraphrased liberally from William Grimes's excellent *Straight Up or On the Rocks*, the first cocktail book ever to be written by a Ph.D.). The late 1940s were a depressing time for fogeys like cocktail theorist David Embury, who waited in vain for their beloved long-aged, straight whiskeys to come back. Nobody else seemed to care. They were happy with the blends. And once the fellas in marketing figured out that people were tolerating this whiskey lite—"whiskey-flavored alcohol," Embury called it—just fine, it was the work of a moment to turn a frown upside down. Not much flavor? That's a good thing. That means it's, ah, smoother. Better.

Meanwhile, back in 1934 a Ukranian immigrant named Rudolf Kunett had bought the U.S. rights to the French Smirnoff brand (formerly, of course, Russian, until the hugger-mugger with the Bolsheviks) and started making and marketing vodka in America. Now, we had heard of the stuff, to be sure. Alas for Kunett, it wasn't that we didn't know vodka, it was that we really didn't like it much (one 1933 drink book defined vodka as "Russian for 'horrendous'"). There were exceptions—detailed under the **Bloody Mary** and the **Vodka Martini**—but not enough for Kunett to actually turn a profit.

In 1939, an exec at Connecticut's Heublein, Inc. (makers chiefly of bottled cocktails) by the name of John G. Martin convinced them, Lord knows

Iced vodka, with business: dip one side of a thin lemon circle in sugar, the other in ground espresso, down the shot, chew the lemon; it's called a **KGB** (it used to be a **Nicoloscar**, but that was with cognac). ▼

how, to buy Kunett out, for all of 14K. Martin was not a stupid man, although it kinda seemed that way at first. He did happen to catch a couple of lucky breaks. First off, when they bottled up Kunett's remaining stock, they used the leftover corks from his even-less-successful attempt at making whiskey. Heublein's distributor in South Carolina, the story goes, took one look at the cork and came out with the slogan "Smirnoff White Whiskey. No taste. No smell." This, especially when refined into "Smirnoff leaves you breathless," inaugurated vodka's lock on the, ah, dedicated daytime drinker.

The War years were a boomy time for vodka. You could do your patriotic duty while tying one on. The Soviet Union (remember the Commies?) was an ally, after all. Although, most of the vodka around was made in Cuba from sugarcane. At any rate, once the advertising industry convinced Americans that less is better, flavor-wise, vodka's work was done.

It took the distillers no time at all to learn how to water down their column-distilled grain alcohol, filter it and rush it into clear bottles—no need for expensive aging. No need for wood, or coopers (barrel makers) or even warehouses that hold more than a day or two's production. One hundred percent grain neutral spirits, stepped on with a little distilled water. Nothing easier to make, or—it turned out—promote (see the **Moscow Mule**). In 1950, 40,000 cases of vodka were sold. In 1955, 4,000,000. Now *that's* marketing. (It didn't hurt a bit that vodka came from our Cold-War enemy: nothing helps sell a lifestyle product better than a touch of transgression.) In 1967, vodka outsold gin. In 1976, it outsold whiskey.

These days, one out of every four bottles of liquor sold in this country is vodka. We suspect that proportion's a lot higher among the generations who are good at video games. Frankly, as you will have picked up by now, we're not very happy about that. We don't dislike vodka, but we don't like it, either—there's not very much there to like. As a mixer, the way most people drink it, it adds proof and nothing else, traveling among the other ingredients like a secret agent, detectable only when there has been a miscalculation, a failure of tradecraft.

Rye, in the meantime, just withered away. By the 1970s, if you ordered it in a bar you'd get Canadian whiskey (blended, natch)—all they had. They even stopped carrying it at New York's P.J. Clarke's, the joint where Ray Milland sank all those ryes in *The Lost Weekend*. The consolidated distillers that had come to dominate the whiskey biz kept a couple of brands around— decent but uninspiring mixing-grade whiskies no more than four years old, where even an average pre-Prohibition brand such as Red Top Rye could boast of ten years in wood. They were an afterthought, a way of picking up a little pocket change from the handful of Lucky-Strike smokers who'd rather quit than switch. There was no attempt at advertising, promotion, distribution.

Bourbon, of course, managed to pull through the Early Plastic Age in much better shape. Why? It has to do with a lot of stuff too sensitive to get into in a drink book.

THE NEXT AGE

Bourbon and even rye have been making something of a comeback lately, in the guise of connoisseur's drinks. That doesn't change the fact that whiskey's days in America are essentially done, at least as far as popular drinking goes. This, we believe, is only just. Whiskey is a noble spirit. We yield to nobody in our admiration for it. Yet bourbon and especially rye have an element of stiff-necked agrarian pride in them that doesn't sort well with America as we know it. Despite the popularity of stock-car racing and the W.W.F., our America is a cosmopolitan country. The guy in the Austin 3:16 shirt is as likely to have been born in Matamoros as in Mayberry. Our America is as likely to be cruising down the road in its Lexus, blasting Cuban music and gangsta rap with an order of takeout Thai noodles on the seat beside it as it is to be sitting in its Ford F-150 listening to Alan Jackson on the AM and eating ribs from Dougie's Drive-Thru Bar-B-Que.

There's only one spirit that can cover all those bases. Rustic and sophisticated, familiar and exotic, light and flavorful, eminently mixable and able to stand alone, the distilled essence of sugarcane can offer itself as all things to all people and yet retain a dignity, even a peculiar nobility, of its own (unless, of course, it's been spiced). Puritan vodka versus catholic-with-a-lowercase-c rum—that's the choice. We're betting on the old-timer.

The proper use
of the shaker:
achieving cocktail
liftoff requires
maximum thrust.

…AND HOW TO MIX IT:

Fundamentals of the Metaphysics of Mixology

IF WE'RE NOT SURE WHEN the first cocktail was poured, we at least know when the first cocktail hour was. In A.D. 77, Pliny the Elder, a Roman who thought he knew everything there was to be known and tried to write it all down (yeah, one of those), noted that forty years before, during the reign of the Emperor Tiberius, "*institutum ut ieiuni biberent potusque uini antecederet cibos.*" In English: "it was established that people might drink on an empty stomach and wine-drinking could come before meals." Is that decadence or civilization?

Leaving such questions for the moral historians, let us but observe that the hour of preprandial bibbing had to wait some 1700 years to achieve its full potential, with the invention of the cocktail. For reasons that are fully understandable, nobody's sure exactly when or where this momentous event occurred (theories abound, all merest guesswork). But, in America, it was around the time we tore ourselves loose from the grasping fingers of George III. In 1806, the cocktail made it into print; see the **Old-Fashioned** for further details.

Before the cocktail, folks mixed drinks, sure. But they were puny, weak, sweet, watery, heavy—nothing like the frozen lightning-bolt that is our birthright. (Well, some of 'em were pretty good, if you like punches. Which we do.) But rather than provide a general history of the mixed drink, we've parceled out our lore and observations among the individual drinks contained in Part II of this book, which we suggest you consult with minimum delay.

There is, however, a (slender) theoretical aspect to "the fine art of mixing drinks," as mixologist David Embury dubbed it, which we cannot ignore. A proper drink, be it a cocktail, a **Highball** or a bowl of punch, is balanced, with no one ingredient imposing its unchallenged will on all the others—it is a democracy, not a dictatorship. If there is sour, there must be sweet, if sharp and aromatic, mellow and rounded. Furthermore, a good drink, like a democracy, must be open in its doings. You should be able to taste the liquor in it (but not so much that you have to pull a face and rush it past a complaining palate). A drink whose power is self-evident demands respect and encourages moderation in those who approach it. A drink should taste only like itself, not like bubblegum or iced tea or one of the beverages of childhood. A drink should be mixed for the tongue, not the eye. Mixing drinks isn't a performing art. It's a craft.

EQUIPMENT

Barware. There's an awful lot of bar gear on the market, both new and vintage. Most of it is unnecessary. You can shake a drink in an old coffee can and serve it in a jelly jar, if you have to, and it'll still taste great if you've used good ingredients and paid attention to the proportions. Some of it is just plain bad. In general, though, here's what you'll need.

Glassware There are approximately 572 different kinds of drink glass. Of these, you really need only three or four. A thin-sided, stemmed cocktail glass, holding 4 to 6 oz (the thin-sidedness means it'll chill faster, and the stem keeps warm hands away from cold booze). A tall, narrow-mouthed Collins glass, holding 10 to 16 oz (the narrow mouth keeps fizzy drinks from going flat too quickly). A short, heavy-bottomed Old-Fashioned glass, holding 6 to 8 oz (the heavy bottom helps when you're muddling things in the glass). A 3 or 4 oz glass for straight liquor or liqueurs. We're not going to make suggestions beyond that. Let taste and common sense decide. If you prefer your **Sazerac** in a Delmonico glass (a 6 oz slant-sided, narrow tumbler), drink it in a Delmonico glass. Buy what you like.

Jigger If you're going to be measuring your ingredients, which we strongly recommend, you're going to need something to measure them with. The standard two-sider, with the (larger) jigger and (smaller) pony back-to-back, is a beautiful thing—if you get the right size. Many jiggers that you find supply a piker's measure of 1¼ oz, with a ¾ oz pony (according to one old drink book, this was "used in the financial district of New York City from 1880 to 1919"). The slightly-larger 1½ oz jigger is better; most drink books base their recipes on this measure. We here at *Esquire*, however, find this wanting. To quote Charles H. Baker, Jr., the Jacques Cousteau of drink writing, "a jigger less than 2 oz is both unthinkable and an insult to all guests." And in fact, when the jigger first turned up as a unit of mixology, it was 2 oz (see, for example, George J. Kappeler's 1895 *Modern American Drinks*). We've jiggered our formulae accordingly. (The 2-oz stainless-steel jigger you'll find in restaurant supply stores has a 1-oz pony; sometimes you can also find a 3-oz/1½-oz graduated plastic version that allows you to measure just about any quantity you'll need.)

Juicer Unless you're such a fogey that you won't allow fruit juice anywhere near good liquor, you'll need something to extract the stuff from various limes, lemons, oranges and grapefruit. The standard kitchen-type reamer works okay, although it can be a pain if you've got a lot of juicing to do (if you're lazy, they make electric ones). We prefer, however, the kind of juicer that works by squeezing, not reaming—that way, less of the bitter pith gets

▲ **The standard cocktail (a.k.a. Martini)** glass, with assorted tall glasses looking on.

into the drink. There are numerous versions of these, ranging from the $100 heavy-duty pro model to the flimsy tin hand-model that squishes the half-fruit from the sides. Our favorite for everyday use is the so-called 'Mexican squeezer', where you put your half-fruit face down in a little perforated cup and lever another cup into its back. Very effective, if too small for oranges and grapefruits.

Measuring spoons   The standard stainless kitchen-spoon set works fine. Make sure you've got at least a tablespoon, a half-tablespoon, a teaspoon and a half-teaspoon.

Miscellaneous   A *knife*. A *muddler*—a hardwood dowel for mushing sugar, lemons and limes in the glass; these are almost impossible to find anymore, and when you do find them they're varnished (do you want varnish in that **Caipirinha**?). In other words, be creative. *Ice tongs* and *insulated bucket* (make sure the bucket has a raised, perforated bottom, to keep the ice from stewing in its own runoff). A *long-handled barspoon*. An *ice bag* and *mallet*. A heavy-duty blender, if you're going to make frozen drinks. (See the Ice section on page 41.)

Shaker   There are all kinds of cute cocktail shakers out there, made from just about anything you can imagine, in just about every shape you can imagine. Save those for the mantlepiece. Mixing drinks is serious business, and that demands serious equipment: large, simple, steel. It should hold at least 16 ounces, be easy to clean, and the top shouldn't leak. Silver looks nice, but it tarnishes and is easy to dent. Aluminum reacts with acids (that **Daiquiri** will taste like Reynolds Wrap). Glass is a poor conductor of heat—much of your ice will be working to cool it, not the drink (plus, the tops of glass shakers always seem to leak). Don't worry about the built-in pourer or strainer; you won't be using that.

Strainer   The tiny strainer that's built into most cocktail shakers is essentially useless: while you're waiting for the drink to filter through it, your ice is busily melting away, reducing your tipple to water. You need a cocktail strainer. The kind that fits in the standard mixing tin is a 'Hawthorn' strainer—one of those paddle-shaped devices with a spring around the edge that fits over the top of the shaker. The spring rim allows for a tight fit, but not too tight.

MIXERS

Mixed drinks contain more than just liquor. Here, briefly, is the other stuff.

Aromatics This is the term of art for herbed, fortified wines, such as vermouth, Dubonnet, Lillet, and the like. There are dozens of these, almost all made in Italy or France, where they are traditionally taken as an *apéritif*—a 'stomach-opener'—in the blue hour before dinner. In America, of course, that's when you have a **Martini**.

At one time or the other, every single one of these fortified wines has been mixed with gin in an effort to improve the **Martini**, as if that were necessary. For general cocktail use, however, vermouth remains king of the hill. There are two styles: Italian, or sweet, which is red, and French, or dry, which is white—off-white, anyway. You can buy an 'Italian' vermouth that's made in France, and a 'French' vermouth that's made in Italy—or California, for that matter. If possible, vermouth should be kept in the refrigerator. The stuff doesn't quite have enough alcohol in it to preserve it indefinitely once it's been opened. Besides, your cocktails will turn out colder.

Bitters Every bar worthy of the name used to keep a full array of little shaker-topped bottles full of bitters to point up their drinks. Manhattan bitters. Abbott's bitters. Boker's, Pepsin, Pomelo, the list went on. Of these, the most important by far was the one with the orange bitters. Once omnipresent (they turn up in 104 of the 284 cocktails in *The Old Waldorf-Astoria Bar Book*—the Social Register of American mixology) and now as rare as buggy whips, orange bitters were the catalyst that tied together many a delightful mixture, from the **Hearst** to the **Suburban** to the **Tuxedo**.

Luckily, they have not entirely vanished; there are Fee Brothers' West Indian Orange Bitters, last survivors of a noble race. Almost as rare are New Orleans's own Peychaud's bitters, without which you can't make a **Sazerac**—our definition of a disability. (See Last Call on page 188 to order either of these.) On the other hand, you can pick up a bottle of Angostura bitters almost anywhere, for which we offer thanks to the benevolent gods and tip out a precious drop of our **Manhattan**.

Citrus Lemons, limes, oranges (and, to a lesser extent, grapefruits) are far and away the most important fruits for making drinks. Their delicate flavor blends well with liquor, while their acidity, in its need to be tamed, promotes all sorts of creative fiddling with sweeteners. Always squeeze your own, though, and use the juice as soon as possible—its flavor will begin to degenerate within a couple of hours.

Before squeezing your citrus fruit, you should 'roll' it—bear down on it while rolling it back and forth on a hard surface—to break the juice cells inside. An average-sized lime yields about 1 oz juice, a lemon a little more; an orange is good for about 2 oz. We don't know what you can squeeze out of a grapefruit. Orange juice is sweet enough to require no added sugar. Lemon and lime juice, however, need at least 1 teaspoon of sugar, syrup or liqueur per ounce to make them palatable, grapefruit juice—hell, who knows? Maybe we shoulda mixed more drinks with grapefruits.

Eggs and Egg Whites Some winter drinks call for raw eggs and some cocktails and fizzes call for raw egg whites. When Shakespeare has Falstaff tell Bardolph "I'll no pullet sperm in my brewage," we doubt he was thinking of salmonella. But these days, we do, so consider yourself forewarned. If you don't want to risk it, you could probably try using some pasteurized substitute; let us know how it turns out. Unless you're making **Eggnog** or **Tom and Jerry**, you can also omit the egg entirely—it won't really affect the flavor much.

Should you press on, you'll find that a little egg white adds opacity, body and a nice head to a drink. Generally, one white—about a tablespoon—is sufficient for two drinks (there's a handy gadget for separating white from yolk, which is more sanitary than using the shell the old-fashioned way). If you're planning to make a raft of egg-white drinks, separate the eggs in advance and whip the whites lightly with a fork or else you'll never be able to measure them properly or even get them out of the damn container—especially after the first round.

Fizz Naturally carbonated water is, literally, as old as the hills. In 1789, the Swiss firm of J. Schweppe figured out how to fake it, on a commercial scale. (Or was it 1794? Accounts differ.) Their soda water was a sensation. These days, club soda, which has soda (as in baking-), and seltzer, which doesn't, are more or less interchangeable, as far as taste goes. They both have more bubbles than the natural stuff, and more than the fizzwater you make in a soda siphon with CO_2 cartridges (although that does have its uses; see the **Fizzes**).

As for soda pop. Rather than use a lemon-lime soda, roll your own: squeeze the fruit, sweeten it and add bubbly water, simple as that. Add hooch and it's called a **Collins**. Ginger ale, on the other hand, is a pain to replicate with fresh ingredients. But ginger ale has been made with artificial flavors since the late-nineteenth century (it was first sold around 1820), so don't worry about finding the authentic stuff. In any case, it's delicately flavored, not too sweet, and very different from ginger beer, which has a lot more ginger in it. Whether you're laying in fizzwater or soda pop, avoid the half-gallon scuba bottle; it'll go flat before you get through it. Liter bottles give you the best balance of economy and bubble-retention.

Finally, there's champagne. It doesn't have to be French, or expensive, but, for cocktail use, it does have to be *dry*—'brut', as it's known.

Garnishes Some mixologists place great importance in the garnish, often more than in the drink itself. Not us. We're not saying a drink shouldn't be allowed to accessorize, but not every drink has to have that extra something. The garnish should contribute something to the drink, and not serve merely as a source of cuteness or 'flair.'

Olives, cocktail onions and maraschino cherries are basically self-explanatory. The standard supermarket kinds work fine for us, but if you want to fiddle with fancy variations, go ahead (but remember the Bogart test). The maraschino cherry, we should note, was already being ranked on as 'made of celluloid' in 1902. Also, if you're building that drink for us, we'd rather you didn't contaminate it with the brine or syrup the garnish is packed in.

Ice Without ice, there is no cocktail. The best way to get ice to release its coldness into a drink is to smash the cubes up before you use them. If your freezer doesn't do this automatically, you'll need an ice bag and mallet. While these are available commercially, they aren't easy to find. The bag is so simple, however, you could practically make one yourself by folding a long strip of clean, new canvas almost all the way back on itself and having someone sew up the sides (worst comes to worst, you can get by with sacking the ice

Whatever you do, don't skimp on the ice.

up in a clean towel). Put the ice cubes in, hold the flap closed and wail away as if your boss' Rolex were inside. Crushing the ice releases almost as much tension as the ensuing drinks.

Your ice should always be reasonably fresh, and as cold as you can get it. It should also be dry—don't leave it to soak in its own melt. And never, ever reuse it for the next round. If you're making **Piña Coladas** or other blender creations, either use crushed ice or feed in the cubes through the hole in the top one or two at a time, about four to six per drink. We don't have to tell you to keep your hand over the hole, do we? Nah.

Liqueurs The most important liqueurs for cocktails fall under the category of curaçao. Originally, there were two kinds: orange and white. Both were flavored with bitter-orange peel, but the orange was built on a brandy base (preferably aged) and heavily sweetened, while the white was distilled to a higher purity, and had the name *triple-sec*—'thrice-dry'—attached to it, for reasons that remain obscure (it's no dryer than the orange kind). Each of these styles is represented by a great nineteenth-century brand: Grand Marnier (made since 1880) is an orange curaçao, with—extravagance!—a cognac base, while Cointreau (1849) is a *triple-sec*. If you can afford them, use them.

Then there are the fruit brandies, which—as further confirmation that people who drink shouldn't be in charge of nomenclature—come in two species, unsweetened *eaux-de-vie* distilled from the fruit, and sweetened grape alcohol flavored with the fruit. Most old drink recipes don't specify which apricot brandy to use—it's a judgment call. Then there's maraschino, distilled from a mash of Dalmatian cherries, but then heavily sweetened; there's always someone. If you can find it, use the Luxardo.

In any case, many makers offer full lines of the standard curaçaos, fruit brandies and *crèmes*—*de menthe*, *de cacao*, etc. Of these, we prefer the French Marie Brizard, the Italian Stock and the Dutch Bols. When it comes to herbal liqueurs, the main ones—Chartreuse (which comes in two colors: green, at 110 proof, and yellow, at 80 proof), Bénédictine, and Drambuie—are long-established premium brands; accept no substitutions. As for absinthe: see the **Absinthe Frappé**, and tell your jet-setting pals to look for the Spanish Absenta Deva brand, or the Mari Mayans, from Ibiza.

Sweeteners Drinks with citrus or bitters are usually sweetened. Sometimes, this is done by adding a liqueur. Usually, though, it's just plain old sugar. If you don't want a little pile of sugar-grit at the bottom of your drink, though, the ordinary granulated white won't do. The easiest solution is to use bar sugar, otherwise known as superfine, instant-dissolving or castor sugar. Make sure to add it before the ice, though, and give it a couple of stirs—sugar dissolves poorly in cold liquids. DO NOT USE POWDERED CONFECTIONERS' SUGAR. It has starch in it. (But then again, if you like your **Whiskey Sours** chunk-style….)

Many mixologists prefer to save themselves the hassle of dealing with granulated sugar and use simple syrup—simply stir two cups sugar and one cup water over medium heat until it boils, remove from heat, skim off any film or scum that forms on top, let cool, and bottle; it will keep in your refrigerator for a long time. Simple syrup, also erroneously known as 'gum' or 'gomme' syrup (which is a different critter; see the **Pisco Punch**), always dissolves and is easy to measure. On the other hand, you have to prepare it in advance, it's really sticky, and you can't substitute it 1:1 for granulated sugar—try using two parts syrup for every part sugar the recipe calls for.

Then there are the flavored syrups. Before Prohibition, every bar kept a full array of soda-fountain syrups: pineapple, raspberry, lemon, like that. The only one still in common use is grenadine, an intensely red business that used to be made from pomegranates and now is made from sugar and chemicals. Don't drink it straight, and remember that a little goes a long way. Other syrups that turn up occasionally are orgeat, which is almond-flavored and also travels under the Italian name *orzata* (you can generally find it in fancy-coffee joints) and Falernum, flavored with lime oil and cane syrup and originally from Barbados; it's particularly good in a rum punch.

The Twist The point of twisting a sliver of orange or lemon peel (lime peel is nasty) over your drink is to get a few microscopic drops of the oil into it. So. Cut a strip of the peel at least an inch long and no more than ¼ inch wide. There are handy bar tools that will carve these out in an instant, or you can use a knife (do it *before* the party). If your twist has some of the pith stuck to it, lay it face down on the counter and shave it off with your knife; the pith

RULE #603

You can always add *more* sugar.

has, let's say, congeners, and not good ones. Hold the twist over the drink rind-side down and, well, twist it. Its work being then complete, you're not supposed to throw it in, but we always do. Weak.

To frost the rim of a glass—a trick that goes back at least to the 1840s, when New Orleans barkeep Joseph Santini used it for his famous Crusta—rub the rim of the glass with a bit of cut lemon or lime and twirl it in bar sugar that's spread out on a plate. The same technique applies to the **Margarita**, except you use coarse salt.

TECHNIQUE, or HOW TO MIX DRINKS:

Tall drinks can generally take care of themselves, but there are a few finer points to mixing cocktails. Take your mixing glass or mixing tin. If the drink has citrus or other juice in it, pour that in (we generally strain ours, through a small-meshed conical kitchen strainer: the drink has a smoother texture, looks better, and everything is much easier to clean without all those bits of dried pulp sticking to it). Some mixologists insist that the ice goes in first, but we disagree: once the ice is in, the fuse is lit. If you put it in last, you don't have to rush and you can adjust for any imbalances.

Then add the sugar or other sweetener and give it a couple of quick stirs. Then everything else, including the liquor (of course, if you don't hold truck with sissy fruit-juice drinks, you'll begin here). Here we'll insert a key piece of advice from Trader Vic, who mixed as many good drinks as anyone ever: "novice or professional, measure your liquor." In fact, measure everything. There's no shame in it. The pour-and-count system used by most bartenders these days is just too inexact in the hands of all but a confirmed expert to make consistently good drinks.

Now the ice. Bernard Devoto, the world's most rabid Martinophile, quotes with approbation his friend's **Martini** recipe which ends "and 500 pounds of ice." He's right; you can never use too much. Go with at least 8 oz per drink (an average home-refrigerator type cube is an ounce). Question: cubed or cracked? Cognoscenti—well, barflies, really—have been known to debate this one with bitterness and vigor. But you can't separate that question from the even more viciously-debated one about shaking versus stirring.

Rather than risk a broken-off bar glass in the eye, we punted the whole thing down to the boys in our Esquire Laboratories.

Now, before we get into the figures, we should note that there are some drinks that everybody agrees you have to shake. Anything with egg white, cream, juice (unless it's canned pineapple juice—always use the unsweetened—which tends to froth excessively) needs to absorb some kinetic energy for the various parts to combine. And you never shake anything fizzy.

Beyond that, let the games begin. When you cut through all the hoo-hah, it all comes down to what you prefer in a drink: strength or coldness. We go with Kingsley Amis, who postulated that "it is more important that a cold drink should be as cold as possible than that it should be as concentrated as possible." If you want mere firepower, stick with iced shots.

For maximum chill, nothing beats stirring with cracked ice. A standard 4-oz drink will be some 3° F (1.7° C) colder stirred with cracked ice than shaken with it; either way, it'll be colder by up to 12° F (6.7° C) than if you use cubed ice, if marginally more dilute (the lab boys say it's a question of a mere quarter-ounce's difference). Plus, a stirred drink will come out clearer than a shaken one, which has thousands of tiny air bubbles beaten into it (some people care about that sort of thing). So stir that **Martini**. James Bond was an idiot.

Whether you shake or stir, ten to fifteen seconds of vigorous activity should do the trick (and we mean vigorous: the standard 'bartender's wiggle' is a manifestation of laziness and decline). Now strain your drink into a chilled glass (the fastest way to chill a glass is to fill it up with cracked ice and top it off with cold water; if you've got five minutes, though, use the freezer—it's easier and it saves on ice). Garnish. You know what to do next.

Yours for a mere $7500, the ultimate patio bar. Do you have to spend the price of a used Honda Civic to mix good drinks? No. But a boy can dream... ▼

PART II:

The

Drinks

A NOTE ON THE RECIPES   *In general, we like our drinks on the dry side, and we've calibrated these accordingly. If they're too tart for you, just add a bit more sugar or liqueur or whatever (easier than making 'em less sweet, no?). No need to fuss. That goes for everything else, too. The first rule for **Drinks***: *'Mix how ya like.' We've made these drinks the way we like 'em; you go forth and do likewise.*

THE MARTINI

Be near me when my light is low,
When the blood creeps, and the nerves prick
And tingle; and the heart is sick,
And all the wheels of Being slow.
—ALFRED, LORD TENNYSON

SHORT DRINKS

A QUICK BLAST of liquor, shaken or stirred until chilled to the bone and promptly inserted in the head. You know, a *cocktail*.

THE FOUR PILLARS OF WISDOM

The four perfect cocktails. Master these and you need never quail before the thirsty eye of a guest.

OLD-FASHIONED

SADLY NEGLECTED THESE DAYS, the Old-Fashioned is the *ur*-cocktail, the father of a prolific and thriving race—few members of which can equal it as a tonic for jangled nerve, and none surpass it.

Now, there's been a lot of nonsense put about over the years concerning Louisville's famous (in the drink world, anyway) Pendennis Club and the invention of the Old-Fashioned, some time in the late 1800s. Responsible for this is a failure of reading comprehension so dire as to call into question the entire American educational system.

The full name of the drink, you see, is the 'Old-Fashioned Whiskey Cocktail', and that's all this is: originally—in 1806, at least, which is good enough for us—a 'cock tail' was a morning drink (ah, America!) made up of a little water, a little sugar, a lot of liquor, and a couple splashes of bitters. Freeze the water (ice started turning up in American drinks in the 1830s), make it with whiskey, and you have the classic Old-Fashioned. (We might be grudgingly brought to accept that the Pendennisites have been blinded to the obvious by the 'traditional' garnish which has been imposed on the drink: the cherry, the orange slice, the pineapple stick. Although if that's what the club contributed to the Old-Fashioned, may it be burnt with fire and all that is therein, saving only the vessels of brass and of iron.)

OLD-FASHIONED

In an Old-Fashioned glass (basically, a small, heavy-bottomed tumbler), place a sugar cube (or ½ teaspoon loose sugar)

Wet this down with 2 or 3 dashes of Angostura bitters and a short splash of water or club soda

Crush the sugar with a wooden muddler, chopstick, strong spoon, lipstick, cartridge case, whatever

Rotate the glass so that sugar grains and bitters give it a lining

Add a large ice cube

Pour in 2½ oz rye or bourbon

Squeeze a twist of lemon over it and serve with stirring rod. If you just can't resist the fruit, for whatever sentimental reasons, at least refrain from the common atrocity of muddling it with the sugar before pouring in the hooch—this turns a noble drink into a sickly, gooey-tasting mess. F.D.R. took his with only a twist, and he led us through depression and war.

The question of whence it hails isn't the only debate surrounding the Old-Fashioned. There's also the question of rye or bourbon. North or South, East or West, Kentucky Colonel or New York Knickerbocker? Frankly, since you can make a fine-tasting drink by subjecting almost any of the manly liquors—brandy, rum, gin, tequila, Irish whiskey (but not Scotch, which is too manly)—to the 'cock-tail' process, it doesn't really matter. But we like an aged rye, if we can find it. Cheap bourbon is already sweet enough, and good bourbon doesn't need any help going down.

But the Old-Fashioned towers above all such quibbling like Gulliver among the Lilliputians. Properly made, without the fruit (an example of the indignities that so many American cocktails had visited upon them under Prohibition; anything to hide the taste of the 'liquor'), this is one of the immortals: strong, square-jawed, with just enough civilization to keep you from hollerin' like a mountain-jack.

ORE HAS BEEN WRITTEN about the Martini than about all of the countries of sub-Saharan Africa, put together. Whole books about it. It has a mystique.

In actuality, though, it is the soul of simplicity: a goodly amount of gin, a splash of vermouth, and a garnish. Shake (or stir) liquids vigorously with ice, strain into a chilled, conical glass and drop in garnish. Nothing to it.

That's the problem. Where mystique and simplicity collide, you get religion. Everyone swears their proportion of gin to vermouth, their choice of garnish, is the only true one; all others are in the way of heresy. Originally—before Prohibition, anyway (the drink probably dates to the 1870s, but nobody's really sure; it's a debate we're happy to stay out of)—it went two parts, or even one part, gin to one part vermouth, with a splash of orange bitters. Garnish: twist of lemon peel. In the thirties, the Stork Club was pouring 'em at five parts gin to one vermouth. At the height of the Martini's powers, in the grey-flannel-suit years, the 'see-through' went something like eight parts gin to no parts vermouth, with an olive. The first is a pleasant tipple, but hardly a Martini; the second, close to perfection. The third is merely iced gin—which is how, if that's what you want, you should have the courage to order it.

As for all the antic combinations that are passing themselves off as Martinis these days. Before fulminating against them, it's worth pausing for a moment to consider the word 'cocktail.' Back in the day—way, way back in the day—

The Martini has made more connections than AT&T. ▼

MARTINI

True disciples, but not fanatics, we hold to this formula:

Stir well with cracked ice:

2 oz London dry gin: Bombay, Booth's, Tanqueray

Scant 2 teaspoons—a little less than ⅓ oz—French vermouth (our preferred ratio, 7:1, is a little tricky to hit with standard measures, unless you like your drinks on the beefy side, in which case go with 3½ oz gin to ½ oz vermouth; but see note below)

Strain into chilled cocktail glass and garnish with twist (if thou wilt walk in the way of the truly righteous, discard even this after extracting its oil). Or with olive—even though it spoils the purity of the drink, which you of course realize, you also know how cool it looks, and how much fun it is to play with.

Note: Better to keep your Martinis on the small side and have two or three than to have one mondo one that gets warm and pungent before you can finish it; with the Martini, coldness is everything.

a cocktail was a particular drink (see the **Old-Fashioned**): liquor, sugar, bitters and water. We're talking around 1800 with this. At the time, there could only have been a few kinds: brandy, rum, whiskey, gin or applejack (in rough order of desirability). Nothing with fruit juice—that includes even lemon juice—could be called a Cocktail; that was a Punch. (Old joke. Innkeeper: "Dost thou take thy cocktail with a twist?" Customer: "Had I desired punch I would have called for punch, damn your eyes!" Badum-sha.) You know what happened next. Folks got to fiddling. Before you know it, there's ice involved. Worse, things like curaçao, almond syrup, absinthe and, yes, lemon juice start loitering in the vicinity, with intent. Eventually, by 1880 or so, a cocktail is anything mixed short, strong and cold. (If you put your foot on the rail and told the nice gentleman with the handlebar mustache, "A cocktail, please," he'd have just stood there. Not enough information.)

A Martini is a cocktail, right? No argument there. So, by similar process of linguistic evolution, that thing in the V-shaped glass with the green-apple schnapps and the raspberry vodka and the ribbon of fruit leather is a Martini. Not a damn thing we can do about it. Language happens.

VARIANTS & MIXOLOGY

If you garnish your Martini with a cocktail onion, it becomes a **Gibson** (although this was originally made with Plymouth gin; try it, the stuff is still around). If you should happen to have some excess absinthe on hand, a couple of drops will transform that Gibson into a **Third Degree** (the driest of the traditional Martini variants, with a ratio of 7:1). And if you do find that Plymouth gin, mix it 2:1 with French vermouth, tip in a couple dashes of orange bitters, and you've got a **Hoffman House**—with a twist, please (New York's Hoffman House, on Twenty-fourth Street across from Madison Square, was famous for the stupendous nakedness of its bar nude and the superlative quality of its drinks; in fact, this is our favorite Martini variant, although we make ours with about 5:1).

Truly reckless mixologists will take your standard 2:1 dry Martini and serially double-dash in orange bitters, maraschino and absinthe, not omitting our old friend the olive. That's a **Turf**, just so you'll know what to avoid. And if you really like to live dangerously, there exists the Italian vermouth alternative; for that, see the **Hearst**.

MANHATTAN

WHEN PROPERLY BUILT, the Manhattan is the only cocktail that can slug it out toe-to-toe with the Martini. It's bold, fortifying and yet as relaxing as a deep massage. J.P. Morgan used to have one at the close of each trading day. It's that kind of drink.

"When properly built"—there's the problem. For a real Manhattan, you need rye whiskey. No amount of fiddling with the vermouth and bitters can save this drink if you've got bourbon in the foundations; it's just too sticky-sweet. But with that rye, this venerable creation— its roots stretch back to the old Manhattan Club, in 1874—is as close to divine perfection as a cocktail may come. The harmony between the bitters, the sweet vermouth and the sharp, musky whiskey rivals even that existing between gin and tonic water.

All things change, and immortality is not in the grasp of man or his creations. For many a year, it seemed that the virtual disappearance of rye meant that the real Manhattan had gone the way of the Aztecs. Luckily, that's not the end of the story. The wave of high living that washed us out of the last century has brought with it a renewed interest in fine, funky old things like cigars, big-band jazz and rye whiskey. Sure, sometimes this gets carried to extremes, but if that means that nobody will ever again pour a bourbon Manhattan, we'll gladly put up with all the dipshits in "Make Mine with Rye" T-shirts.

RULE #823

If the bartender can't make a decent **Manhattan**, that "house special" will probably suck, too.

Mr. Morgan calls for strong drink. ▶

MANHATTAN

Stir well with cracked ice:

2 oz good rye (we like the 101-proof Wild Turkey for this, but it's also good with Jim Beam, Old Overholt, Van Winkle Family Reserve or Sazerac, moving up the price scale); in case of emergency—you need a Manhattan and you're passing a bar of the "Rye? Nah." variety—Canadian Club will do (it's got a lot of rye in it)

1 oz Italian vermouth (Martini & Rossi is both traditional and excellent)

2 dashes Angostura bitters or orange bitters (the old Waldorf-Astoria used orange)

Strain into in chilled cocktail glass and garnish with twist or, of course, maraschino cherry—subject to the same reservations attending olives and **Martinis**.

VARIANTS & MIXOLOGY

Human beings, being human beings, can never leave well enough alone. Here, then, the obligatory variants. A few you can make by monkeying around with the bitters: lose the Angostura and pitch in a splash of Amer Picon and it's a **Monahan Special** (Mike Monahan tended bar at the old Waldorf-Astoria); a splash of anisette and it's a **Narragansett**; two dashes of cherry brandy and a dash of absinthe and you've got a **McKinley's Delight**. Leave a dash of the Angostura in, add a dash of orange bitters and *three* dashes of absinthe: a **Sherman**.

Or you can tinker with the vermouth. Replace half the Italian vermouth with French for a so-called **Perfect Manhattan**. Equal parts of rye, French vermouth and Italian vermouth—a **Jumbo** (probably named after Barnum's elephant, who could drink a quart of whiskey without visible effect and died when—sober, they say—he got run into by a train in St. Thomas, Ontario, where they're still trying to live it down); make that with bourbon: a **Honolulu** (no bitters at all in those). Cut the Italian vermouth entirely and make it half-and-half bourbon and French vermouth and that's a **Rosemary**; to turn that into a **Brown University**, just add a couple dashes orange bitters (we wonder what they're drinking up in Providence these days). Coming almost full circle, if you make your classic 2:1 Manhattan with French vermouth instead of Italian and a dash of Amer Picon and one of maraschino, you're in **Brooklyn**. There are more—the **Rob Roy**, for one—but….

M

ANY HAVE CLAIMED CREDIT for the
Daiquiri—Cuban barmen, German princelings,
American mining engineers, what have you.
The claim generally held to be most credible
belongs to the mining engineers, one Jennings Cox
and his pal, Harry E. Stout.

Their story, as it has come
down to us: back in 1896, or 1898,
they were doing something-or-other
for the Spanish-American Iron Co. in
the mountains outside Santiago, Cuba—the
town where Bacardi happened to be made.
The water in the coastal village of Daiquiri
(where they lived) being very bad, they were
forced to both distill it and disinfect it with Bacardi
(once the gin ran out), adding lime juice and sugar for
flavor and chilling it down with ice (made from the distilled water, of course). Now, Cox used to drop in from
time to time at the Venus bar in Santiago, where he took
to ordering his rum this same way. The regulars were
intrigued. Before long, it was "Give us what the *señor* from
Daiquiri is having."

In 1898, the United States Army forcibly removed the
island of Cuba from the King of Spain. This was the
Spanish-American War. Next thing you know,
the Yanquis who were suddenly swarming
all over the place—they landed at several
places, including Daiquiri, on June 22 and

DAIQUIRI

Shake well with cracked ice:

2 oz white rum (Bacardi, an old
Cuban brand, is traditional,
although practically any rum
will do; we, in fact, often prefer a darker, older rum—a
**Jamaica Rum
Cocktail**, as
it's known,
which
becomes
a **Brown
Derby** if
you use
maple sugar
instead of cane)

1 teaspoon bar sugar

Juice of ½ lime

Strain into chilled cocktail glass.

**Daiquiri's somewhere
around here.**

VARIANTS & MIXOLOGY

Once you've got a wonderful invention, wherever it came from, why stop there? Add half an egg white and you've got a **Nugent**, and a nice head. Or you can also replace the sugar with ½ oz honey (or less), making sure to stir the honey in the lime juice until it dissolves before you build the rest of the drink. That's a **Honey Bee**.

But far more interesting than these is the **Daiquiri Number 3**, as served by the justly famous Constantino Ribalaigua, "el Rey de los Cocteleros," at Havana's El Floridita bar: 2 oz Bacardi, 1 teaspoon sugar, juice ½ lime (squeezed by hand over the shaker), 1 teaspoon fresh grapefruit juice, 1 teaspoon maraschino; shake well with cracked ice and strain into a champagne saucer full of shaved ice.

Hemingway liked these without the sugar—and double (the precise **Papa Doble**: "two and a half jiggers Bacardi White Label Rum, the juice of two limes and half a grapefruit, and six drops of maraschino, all placed in an electric mixer over shaved ice, whirled vigorously and served foaming in large goblets"—A. E. Hotchner, *Papa Hemingway*).

occupied Santiago on July 17 after a generally lackluster campaign—adopted this new drink and brought it home with them.

This tale is questionable in so many different ways it's difficult to know where to begin. Ice? In Cuba, in 1896? Now, sure, artificial refrigeration had been around since Ferdinand Carré put it on a sound commercial footing in 1859, but the machines were pretty damn cumbersome and plenty cantankerous, and we'd be very surprised if they had one in squalid little Daiquiri (did they even have electricity there?). One thing's for certain: when the Yanks landed there in 1898, they had to get ice for the wounded from William Randolph Hearst, who was down there in his yacht. And just what were Cox and Stout doing in Cuba, anyway? In 1896, the island was in the midst of a full-scale civil war, and the countryside was no place for a gringo; nor were things much better in 1898, what with the gunfire and the dysentery and the typhoid and the yellow fever and, especially, the malaria.

But those are mere quibbles compared to the real question: what exactly did they invent? Rum, lime juice and sugar have a long history together (see Admiral Vernon's **Lime Grog**). Setting the Royal Navy aside, most Caribbean and South American countries make liquor out of sugar cane, grow limes and drink them together—what's the Brazilian **Caipirinha** but a Daiquiri on the rocks? In fact, the Daiquiri represents such an obvious marriage between native ingredients—rum, sugar, limes, ice (wherever they got it from)—and American technology—the cocktail shaker—that it would take the chowder-headedest duffer who ever buttoned a trouser *not* to invent it. So, Cox and Stout? Just the guys who brought the ice and the shaker. Or maybe just the shaker. And maybe not even that: this Venus bar—if they had something as fancy as ice, they must've had a cocktail shaker, right? And if they weren't mixing the local wet goods in it, what *were* they mixing?

No matter. It's a perfect drink. But we do wonder what Teddy Roosevelt would say if he knew that a mere cocktail named after the "squalid little village" where his Rough Riders landed would live on in the popular memory of his countrymen for decades after T.R.'s little war was effaced as if it had happened before the Flood. Remember the Maine!

GIN COCKTAILS

WILLIAM SEABROOK'S ASYLUM

This one comes down to us from a slim 1935 volume titled *So Red the Nose, or Breath in the Afternoon* (would we make that up?): thirty literary celebrities of the day each contributed a cocktail and a blurb (see **Ernest Hemingway's Death in the Afternoon**). Seabrook, a Hearst man, was chiefly famous for two books. One was a pretty wild account of his time in Haiti, complete with his 'blood baptism' into the sacred mysteries of Voodoo (he was a friend of Aleister Crowley's and all). The other treats of the rather scaly months he spent in the bughouse, self-committed on account of his drinking. He called it (how'd you guess?)...*Asylum*. It is not a bartender's guide.

According to Seabrook, this potion will "look like rosy dawn, taste like the milk of Paradise, and make you plenty crazy." He got one thing right, anyway: too many of these atrocities and they'll zombie-march you straight into the land of buckle-back coats and Thorazine. But it tastes more like the milk of dynamite, and if this is what Seabrook's dawns looked like, he must've been sighting the sun through a pitcher of **Whiskey Sours**.

Yet the Asylum shouldn't be ejected entirely from the pharmacopoeia; it has its uses. Between the Pernod and the gin, you've got the extracts of a few dozen assorted roots and herbs, not a few of which must have some serious juju going for them. In times of direst emergency—girlfriend's night to host poetry circle, sister and no-neck brother-in-law on their way over with the triplets, tax return accidentally mailed to ex-wife's lawyer and alimony check to the IRS, etc.—the Asylum seems to impart a trancelike, unblinking calm that is difficult to otherwise achieve.

BRONX

BRONX

Shake well with cracked ice:

2 oz London dry gin

1 oz orange juice (fresh-squeezed and strained, of course)

½ teaspoon French vermouth

½ teaspoon Italian vermouth

Strain into chilled cocktail glass.

Time was, every borough in New York had to have a cocktail. Well, except for Queens. And Staten Island. But there was a **Brooklyn**, of sorts (fuhgeddabout it), and you all know about the **Manhattan**. That leaves this baby. The Bronx. Its origins are as undisputed as anything involving alcohol can get: Johnnie Solon, Spanish-American War vet and master bartender at the old Waldorf-Astoria (back when that was, for cocktails, *the* bar in *the* city in *the* country), slung it together when a lunchtime customer challenged him to come up with something new. Instant hit.

Solon's formula is at left. We should note, however, that almost nobody seems to have been satisfied with it—nobody who committed his thoughts on mixology to posterity, anyway. Fair enough; opinions will differ. But in this case, all the others are wrong. Every published variation is based on the premise that the drink lacks punch, a fault for which they try to compensate by pumping up the vermouths and letting a little air out of the O.J., sometimes to the point where it's a mere squeeze of peel. This is (ahem) fruitless. No amount of jiggling with figures can toughen this baby up enough for it to compete with, say, the **Manhattan**; it's like trying to make an action hero out of James Dean.

What's more, we can deduce from Solon's account of the creation that the day was most likely a warm one (he named the drink after a trip he had taken to the Bronx Zoo a couple of days before; who goes there in the winter?). If we factor in that it was, you'll recall, lunchtime—the hot part of the day—and the important fact that air conditioning was still just an idea bouncing around in Willis Carrier's fertile little brain, all becomes clear. The Bronx must not be judged as an evening bracer, a proper cocktail, but rather as a midday swelter-tamer. As such, it's delightful: clean, simple and very, very refreshing.

CLOVER CLUB

Esquire, a magazine formerly devoted to writing and drinking in pretty much equal proportions (kinda like a lot of writers, come to think of it)—has always had it in for the venerable Clover Club. The signature tipple of a Philly lawyers' and writers' club of the same name, it was a turn-of-the-century staple. Yeats, of all people, was known to suck 'em down with his dinner. And yet, in 1934 we lumped it together with the 'pansies'—the ten worst cocktails of the previous decade (which, that being the decade of bathtub gin and wood alcohol, is saying something). Our 1949 *Handbook for Hosts* tucks it among the Pink Ladies and Alexanders in the "Something for the Girls" section.

There's more to this than meets the palate. Y'see—as Jack Townsend, President of the Bartenders' Union of New York (where have all the good unions gone?), observed in 1951—"the Clover Club drinker is traditionally a gentleman of the pre-Prohibition school," a "distinguished patron of the oak-paneled lounge." In short, Esky (that's him on page 151). Ritual castration of the father. Freud.

We're pretty sure we've worked all that stuff out. Nobody makes drinks with egg whites anymore, but in this case it's worth a shot—the Clover Club is unusual, tasty, strong, and not at all slimy. It is, however, quite pink; if that challenges your masculinity, replace the raspberry syrup with maraschino for a **Dr. Cook** (said doctor being the bogus polar explorer; we don't know if the drink was named after him before or after his fraudulent ways came to light).

CLOVER CLUB

Shake well with cracked ice:

2 oz London dry gin

White of 1 egg

Juice of ½ lemon

3 dashes raspberry syrup (if you must, substitute grenadine)

Strain into in chilled cocktail glass.

VARIANTS & MIXOLOGY

You may garnish the Clover Club with a mint leaf, but be warned that that turns it into a **Clover Leaf**. And if you want to go girly, it's the work of a moment to turn the Clover Club into that fabled virgin-slayer, the **Pink Lady**: simply replace ½ oz of the gin with applejack and use grenadine for the syrup.

DELMONICO NUMBER 1

Shake well with cracked ice:

¾ oz London dry gin

½ oz brandy

½ oz French vermouth

½ oz Italian vermouth

2 dashes Angostura bitters

Strain into chilled cocktail glass and garnish with twist of orange peel.

DELMONICO NUMBER 1

Back in the days before Prohibition, every restaurant with pretensions had a house cocktail. Of course, they do now, too: things like purslane-infused vodka with a splash of fresh-squeezed quince juice and a stick of candied rhubarb, or a puddle of low-proof rice fermentate—all right, sake—delicately accented with a few drops of God-help-us and adorned with a bit of pickled seaweed. Creative, *si*. Cocktails, no.

Sure, there were plenty of lame house cocktails then, too—ninety percent of just about everything ever being crap—but at least they weren't weird. Or weak. Case in point: the Delmonico Number 1, a mellow, wood-paneled little number without anything in particular to distinguish it beyond good taste and tasting good. But that fits. Delmonico, the New York establishment, or establishments—they went through eleven incarnations, following the money as it moved uptown—that introduced America to the concept of fine dining in public, always placed quality above flash.

We're not sure which of the eleven served up this critter, but if you prodded us at gunpoint (and how likely is that? over a cocktail recipe?) we'd have to go with the one that opened across from Madison Square in 1876, right at the beginning of the golden age of the cocktail.

RULE #612

Have two singles rather than one double; that way your drink will always be cold (and you're less likely to end up drinking a lot of hooch you don't want just because it's in your glass).

GIMLET

> "The bartender set the drink in front of me. With the lime juice it has a sort of pale greenish yellowish misty look. I tasted it. It was both sweet and sharp at the same time. The woman in black watched me. Then she lifted her own glass towards me. We both drank. Then I knew hers was the same drink."

—RAYMOND CHANDLER, *The Long Goodbye*

The Gimlets that draw Marlowe and the dame together are fifty-fifty Rose's and gin—unbearably sweet by today's standards. The 1930 Savoy Hotel bar book—the Gimlet's an English drink, with roots in the Royal Navy (the lime juice)—lists one made that way, drunk on the rocks. It also, however, lists a **Gimblet**, with three parts gin to one part lime juice, shaken together and topped off with soda (then there's the **Gillette**—'Chicago Style'—as found in Tom Bullock's 1917 *Ideal Bartender*, which is simply gin, sugar and lime juice). Combine all these and you get the modern 'Gimlet.

Some movie Marlowe or other; if it's not Bogart, does it really matter who? ▼

VARIANTS & MIXOLOGY

The inevitable variation: replace the gin with white rum, 3 parts to every part of Rose's, dash in a little grenadine, and voila! A **Peg O' My Heart**—commemorating J. Hartley Manners' show of the same name, which opened on Broadway December 20, 1912. Although it beats us what rum and lime juice have to do with the story of a plucky young Irish girl's adventures in the New World.

HEARST

Stir well with cracked ice:

2 oz London dry gin (or Plymouth gin—see caveat on facing page)

1 oz Italian vermouth

Dash of orange bitters

Dash of Angostura bitters

Strain into chilled cocktail glass.

HEARST

Gin. Vermouth. Okay. But soft! Two parts to one? And could that be red vermouth? *Sweet* vermouth? Anathema! Moloch! Spake not the Lord unto us that we may put difference between holy and unholy, between unclean and clean? The Hearst violates a couple of the most sacred tenets of modern mixology. One: vermouth, when combined with gin, is like nitroglycerine—in the tiniest quantities, a beneficial heart-tonic; beyond that, catastrophe. Two: Italian or sweet vermouth must never be allowed to contaminate gin in any quantity whatsoever.

You must be a brave drinker, therefore, to take the first sip of one of these. More than likely, you'll need moral support. You may even need to hold somebody's hand. By the second sip, though, you won't have to. After all the pish-tosh about dryness and **Martinis** and eyedroppers—nay, atomizers!—of vermouth has been pished and toshed, you're left with a perfectly suave cocktail that has nothing of the milquetoast about it.

The *Old Waldorf-Astoria Bar Book* credits this simple gloom-lifter to certain of William Randolph's minions "who were in the habit of dropping in at odd times when assigned to a story in the neighborhood." Probably not more than three times a day, we'll bet.

VARIANTS & MIXOLOGY

If you want to leave the Angostura out, do—but then it's an **Amsterdam** you'll be enjoying. Omit the orange bitters? A Sunshine (but not our **Sunshine**, for which see the rum section). Omit both bitters and bung in an egg white? A **White Elephant**—although in color it's closer to a red squirrel. Temper the Italian vermouth by replacing half of it with French and you've got a so-called **Perfect Martini**, which is fine if you believe that perfection lies in the art of compromise (we like our flesh to be flesh and our fish to be fish).

Orange Blossom

The authorities—the men and women who have devoted their lives to mapping the world of drink—pretty much all hate this one. In December, 1934, for example, *Esquire*'s Frank Shay counted it among the ten worst drinks of the year. Others agreed. A few years later, Bernard DeVoto—the Cult of the Dry Martini's High Priest and Executioner—dissected the problem: during Prohibition, folks took to mixing their bathtub hooch with any kind of juice they could get their hands on, chiefly orange (of course). Vitamin C notwithstanding, this made for some viciously unhealthful tipples. And what, according to DeVoto, made them so regustin'? "Not the gin but the fruit juices so basely mixed with it: all pestilential, all gangrenous, and all vile." For a man of his kidney, bad liquor straight is better than good liquor mixed with anything that ever grew on a tree (except maybe a swizzle stick).

What do we think? We'll easily concede that, served straight up in a cocktail glass, the Orange Blossom is distinctly underwhelming. Yet, paradoxically, if prepared Prohibition-style, with the gin and the juice splashed into a glass over an ice cube or two, there's a certain agricultural simplicity to its preparation that appeals to us. For a long-haul blowout, you're not going to want to be making **Ramos Fizzes**. Whatever its faults, this one's quick, easy, and still better than a **Screwdriver** (a creation of the 1950s which is to the Orange Blossom as the **Vodka Martini** is to the **Martini**).

We've got at least one authority on our side, a gent who has recorded paeans to the Orange Blossom—or, as he calls it, **Gin 'n' Juice**—not once, but twice, with some commercial success. Now, given a choice of mobbin' with Snoop Doggy Dogg or sipping **Martinis** with Bernard DeVoto, we'd rather mob. Truth be told, give us a pocket full of rubbers and some bubonic chronic and we'll drink anything.

ORANGE BLOSSOM

Shake well with cracked ice:

2 oz London dry gin

2 oz fresh-squeezed orange juice

Strain into chilled cocktail glass. (If you're going the Gin 'n' Juice route, it's Collins glass, rocks and supermarket juice. Real G's don't squeeze oranges.)

VARIANTS & MIXOLOGY

There is, we should mention, a competing version of the Orange Blossom that calls for equal parts gin, juice and Italian vermouth. In fact, this was probably the original: thus *The Old Waldorf-Astoria Bar Book*, anyway (it also prints the fifty-fifty version, but as the **Adirondack**). Not that DeVoto would have given a good goddamn. To him, Italian vermouth was almost as profane as those gangrenous fruit juices: "the heathen put it to many uses but we know none for it." Sorehead.

PARADISE

Shake well with cracked ice:

2 oz London dry gin

1½ teaspoons apricot brandy

1 oz fresh-squeezed orange juice

½ oz lemon juice

Strain into chilled cocktail glass.

PARADISE

There's a pleasing element of archaeology to what we do here at the Esquire Institute for Advanced Study in Mixology. Take the strange (okay, not *that* strange) case of apricot brandy. It was trendy, once. Back around 1950, Manhattan's Stork Club—the hottest nightclub in America, in an era when nightclubs were hot—even used it in their Cub Room Special, the Cub Room being the area where they warehoused their V.I.P.s. But to find the real apricot brandy fiends, you would've had to frequent the chic Zebra Room, out in L.A., where the movie folk met the debutantes. Now, movie folk have driven more trends in drink than just about anyone. Some—tequila, vodka—are still with us. This one ain't, even with all the best efforts of Joan Crawford and Hedda Hopper (who, along with the Zebra Room, the perennial Polo Lounge and a passel of other filmland institutions, contributed apricot brandy cocktails to *Bottoms Up*, a rather racy 1951 drink compendium). Nowadays, apricot brandy—which is actually a liqueur—tends to lurk in the back of the liquor cabinet, next to that bottle of oily brown stuff somebody brought you from Bulgaria.

Storkin' it, 1938: Al Jolson (right) lets Walter Winchell and J. Edgar in on the secret. ▼

Just as well? Consider the case of the Paradise, apricot brandy's flagship cocktail, as it were. Unfortunately, if you follow the standard recipes—which agree in calling for equal parts gin, apricot brandy and orange juice—the Paradise is, basically, disgusting: it tastes like it should have codeine in it. Even if you double the gin and pitch in a splash of lemon juice, as the 1930 *Savoy Cocktail Book* suggests, it's not much better. Yet, we believe, the Paradise can be saved. It even *should* be saved, for the same reason that we try to save a rare species of orchid. There's a delicately-perfumed, exotic—even romantic—flower in this drink, just waiting for the magic formula to coax it out. Here's our best effort.

PEGU CLUB

Back when Britain had an empire, the folks whose responsibility it was to run it weren't known for their eagerness to mix with the folks they were lording it over. Hence the Club, an island of anxious, obsessive Brits maintaining their peculiar, distant customs in a sea of people behaving sensibly. Only the Club-members didn't quite see it that way: they were normal, everybody else was somehow deviant. Weird.

Anyway, among all these far-flung outposts, few were farther-flung than Rangoon's Pegu Club, where this delightful cocktail was created sometime before 1930, when it turned up in the *Savoy Cocktail Book*. On March 7, 1942, a hundred years almost to the day after they occupied it, the British abandoned Rangoon in the face of the rapidly-advancing Japanese 33rd Infantry Division (they would've held it, see, but curaçao stocks were running dangerously low and the lime situation was perilous…). The British came back in 1945, but the Club was never the same. Now it's a barracks for the Burmese Army. We don't know what they're drinking.

PEGU CLUB

Shake well with cracked ice:

2 oz London dry gin

¾ oz orange curaçao

¾ oz lime juice

Dash Angostura bitters

Dash orange bitters

Strain into chilled cocktail glass.

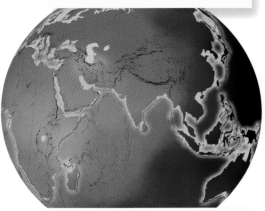

PINK GIN

Along with the **Brandy and Soda,** one of the foundational beverages of the British Empire. If you really, *really* like gin, this staple of the officers' wardroom is as good a way as any to have it. Almost as good, anyway. And it certainly goes a ways towards explaining how an island off the coast of Europe ended up ruling one-fourth of the earth's land surface. Let's just say it's not for the faint-hearted.

To be a truly insufferable twit, step up to the bar and loudly order a **Gin Pahit** ('pa-heet', that being the Malay word for 'bitter'), feigning surprise at your bartender's inevitable ignorance and explaining to all and sundry that that's what everybody was drinking when you were 'out East.' Then again, asking for a Pink Gin's bad enough.

PINK GIN

Splash a few generous drops of Angostura bitters into an Old-Fashioned glass

Roll them around until the inside is coated, pour out the excess, pour in 2 oz London dry gin

Stir.

Americans and other utterly wet types may add an ice cube or two, but then you'll never stiffen that upper lip.

RED LION

Shake well with cracked ice:

1½ oz London dry gin (Booth's, in the original)

1½ oz Grand Marnier

¾ oz fresh-squeezed orange juice

¾ oz lemon juice

Strain into a chilled cocktail glass that has had its rim rubbed with lemon juice and dipped in sugar.

Up the gin by half an ounce and replace the Grand Marnier with an ounce of Cointreau and it's a **Maiden's Prayer**, which is, our 1949 *Handbook for Hosts* comments, "served on the edge of the couch"—a date-peeler, as the name suggests. The modern equivalent, our culture having moved beyond such verbal (or mixological) subtleties, is the Leg Spreader, for which formulae vary to the point of anarchy. They're all disgusting, though. And strong.

RED LION

We owe this simple, urbane little time-waster to one Arthur Tarling, of London's Café Royal. In 1933, he won first prize with it in a London cocktail competition. In fact, the Red Lion has the distinction of being probably the only such contest-winner ever to enter the standard cocktail lists. Lesson?

ROSE

An easygoing old dame who packs a brick in her handbag. She used to be quite popular at the old Waldorf-Astoria.

ROSE

Stir well with cracked ice:

2 oz London dry gin

⅔ oz (½ oz plus 1 teaspoon) Grand Marnier

Strain into a chilled cocktail glass.

TUXEDO

The Tuxedo Club was the first "planned environment for gracious living" in America. In the fall of 1885, Pierre Lorillard IV, of the tobacco Lorillards, took a piece of spare real estate about 35 miles out the Erie Railroad from Jersey City known as "the Wood Pile"—it supplied wood to the railroad—and there did his pleasure-dome decree. Nine months later, it was ready: a huge clubhouse, miles of new roads banked by fieldstone walls, a train station, sewers and other services, and a raft of cottages available by the season to the well-heeled (subject to approval by the club); there was even some discrete housing for the peons. Oh yeah, it was no longer the Wood Pile, a name which simply wouldn't do. As always in the Northeast, there was a convenient Indian name lying around unused: "Tucseto." (The "x" looks much spiffier, don't you think?)

Anyway, on June 16, 1886, the Tuxedo Club opened. Seven hundred guests, all very very. A few months later, at the club's first Autumn Ball, a covey of the younger set—Pierre's son and his buds—thought they'd ruffle the stuffed shirts a bit by chopping the tails off their dress coats. The Prince of Wales, a fashion-forward type, had taken to wearing a short jacket when he was in the country, and this Tuxedo place was the country, so. . . it caught on.

The tail-chopping was about the last wild thing that happened up there. Quoth Emily Post, in 1911: "Old Tuxedoites are very conservative. Unlike the Newporters, Tuxedo people are not living from excitement to excitement. Tuxedo men are hard-working business men who take a 7:40 or an 8:15 train every morning of the week." Ms. Post doesn't say what train they took home, but we'll bet it wasn't the first—they had to make a little time to drop by the Waldorf-Astoria bar (William Waldorf Astor was a Tuxedoite) and drain a couple of these.

Like the denizens of its namesake, the drink—a variation on the **Martini**—is an unostentatious hard-worker: potent, bone-dry, and lacking in the gaudy herbal notes one finds in vermouth. Yet the sherry imparts just a hint of elegant nuttiness that mellows the gin without masking it, and the orange bitters suggest that there may yet be a twinkle in the old gent's eye.

TUXEDO

Shake well with cracked ice:

2 oz London dry gin (For authenticity's sake, use Plymouth gin, although informed sources suggest that today's formula isn't exactly that of yesteryear)

1 oz dry (fino) sherry

Dash of orange bitters

Strain into a chilled cocktail glass.

Note: There are other Tuxedo cocktails out there, but this one appears to be the original, and is certainly the best (although the one Tom Mahoney of the Hoffman House published in 1912, 50-50 French vermouth and Old Tom gin, with dashes of maraschino, absinthe and orange bitters, may have gotten there first).

WHITE LADY

Shake well with cracked ice:

2 oz London dry gin

½ oz Cointreau

½ oz lemon juice

White of 1 egg

Strain into chilled cocktail glass.

WHITE LADY

1919. The most horrifying war so far in history has ended, brought to a halt not by courage, or will, or intelligence, but by exhaustion and the national anemia that inevitably results from losing, say, half a million men in a single battle. Europe wants nothing more than to forget, to pick up where things left off. But it's not so easy—everything's gotten out of whack, somehow, and there's an almost ghoulish edge to the nightlife.

Case in point, the White Lady. Invented by Harry MacElhone, bartender at the superchic Ciro's Club, London and late of His Majesty's forces (and New York's Plaza Hotel bar before that), the White Lady is an unhealthy blend of Cointreau (⅔), crème de menthe (⅙) and lemon juice (⅙). It's the color of chlorine gas and sweet as the smell of death.

Ten years later, and healing has begun to occur. MacElhone has his own place, now: Harry's New York Bar, in Paris. Hemingway, everybody drinks there (still do, as a matter of fact). And he's gotten over his shell shock (what else could have induced a competent mixologist to create a drink with two liqueurs and no liquor?). As token of this, he returns to the White Lady, and makes a decisive, life-affirming change: the crème de menthe is out, gin is in, and the Cointreau is cut back to a healthy level. Of course, now there's an egg white, which makes the drink look a little like decomposing flesh. Every wound must leave its scar.

▲ **Postwar mixology, round two (1949): Harry MacElhone (left) composes his liquid ode to the victors, the Big Four—⅓ rye (for America), ⅓ Scotch (for Britain), ⅙ vodka (for Russia), ⅙ dry vermouth (for France), dash of cherry liqueur (for—well, for why the hell not?).**

VARIANTS & MIXOLOGY

There's another version of the White Lady that replaces the lemon juice with white crème de menthe, multiplies the Cointreau by four, adds ½ oz of brandy and omits the gin entirely. If you're going to call that a White Lady, you might as well call a **Manhattan** a **Martini**.

WHISK(E)Y COCKTAILS

ALGONQUIN

New York's Hotel Algonquin baptized several cocktails in its name, for the most part with pretty shaky results (rum, blackberry brandy and Bénédictine? Nah). This may have been one of 'em, although nobody seems to be sure. In any case, it's fairly unlikely the wits of the famous Round Table grazed on it. Strictly a **Highball** crowd, as we read them, with the occasional **Martini**. Not a bad drink, though.

BRAIN-DUSTER

The combination of whiskey, Italian vermouth and absinthe travels under several names. At the old Waldorf-Astoria, it was honored as the **Waldorf** or the **Hearn's** (history is silent as to whether it was named thus after the Irish-Greek writer and Japanophile Lafcadio Hearn, or some bartender; but in either case the advice which *Esquire*'s 1949 *Handbook for Hosts* attached to it is sound: "hold your hat"). However, it's the earliest recognizable formula we've been able to find—printed in 1895, by George Kappeler—that speaks the most truth about this drink, when it calls it the Brain-Duster. It's the absinthe, of course.

RULE #29

A cocktail is no substitute for a decent education—and vice-versa.

ALGONQUIN

Stir well with cracked ice:

2 oz rye whiskey

1 oz French vermouth

1 oz pineapple juice

Strain into chilled cocktail glass.

BRAIN-DUSTER

Stir well with cracked ice:

1 oz straight rye or bourbon (use something around 100 proof for maximum efficiency)

1 oz absinthe (we recommend the Spanish Absenta brand, although any real—that is, illegal—brand should work; failing that, one of the high-proof legal substitutes is worth a try: it will produce a suitably potent libation but one lacking in that savage something which the adventurous drinker seeks out)

1 oz Italian vermouth

Dash of Angostura bitters

Strain into chilled cocktail glass.

Note: If using absinthe of home production, halve the amount. Trust us. Some insist that if it's a Hearn's you be after, it's Irish whiskey you'll be needin'.

BRAINSTORM

Stir well with cracked ice:

2 oz Irish whiskey

½ tablespoon French vermouth

½ tablespoon Bénédictine

Strain into chilled cocktail glass and garnish with twist of orange peel.

If you're sipping one of these after dinner, probably better to build it on the rocks (it'll stay cold longer): just pour the ingredients into an Old-Fashioned glass, add a couple ice cubes and give it a stir. Even better, turn it into a so-called **Mist** by packing the glass with crushed ice (you should probably shake everything together first, but without ice); serve it with two short straws.

BRAINSTORM

There aren't a hell of a lot of good cocktails based on Irish whiskey. Maybe it's due to the slightly smoky taste, which tends to dominate (although not nearly so much as that of Scotch, and people have managed to come up with a number of fine Scotch drinks; see the next page). Or maybe—this is what we think, anyway—it's due to the tenacious hold the Irish in America have maintained on their ancestral drinking traditions. Even though many of our most celebrated bartenders—Johnnie Solon of the old Waldorf-Astoria (see the **Bronx**), Patrick Gavin Duffy of the Ashland House (inventor of the **Highball**)—have been sons of the Auld Sod, who goes into an O'Connor's or a McSwiggan's today and orders anything more elaborate than a pint and a shot? You'd feel like a tool. But just order that Guinness and that taste of John Power's (or Old Bushmill's, or Tullamore Dew, or Jameson's, or—damn it, we're salivating) and bask in the approval of the establishment.

And a fine thing that is. But there are other things, good things, you can do with Irish whiskey besides absorb it in 1½-ounce doses. And the Brainstorm (a.k.a. the **Antrim**)—a recipe of obscure but venerable origins—is one of the best. The herbal pungency of the Bénédictine points up the malty smoothness of the whiskey, the dryness of the vermouth balances the sweetness of the Bénédictine, and the orange peel adds a hint of sunshine. This one makes an especially fine after-dinner drink.

Scotch whisky does not readily lend itself to cocktails: there's a prickly, stiff-necked pride to the stuff that makes it unwilling to blend. There are exceptions (well, the **Rob Roy**, anyway, and the **Scotch Highball**), but in general, they suck. Most of 'em, it's safe to say, are Prohibition flim flams, ways to tart up the only stuff that was flowing freely. (Before the Great Experiment, Scotch wasn't particularly popular on these shores: to order it in a bar more or less marked one as a weak-wristed, Limey-loving, cake-eater. Once good rye and bourbon got scarce, the gents were more willing to compromise their standards of masculinity.)

Which brings us to the little-known Chancellor. All the standard sources are silent on where it comes from, but we wouldn't be a bit surprised to find it making its maiden voyage around the Fellows' table of one of the less hide-bound Scottish colleges, 'Chancellor' being what they call the presidents of their universities over there. Or you might find it in the Mess Book of the Queens Own Cameron Highlanders or some such prop of the old Empire; those chaps always had plenty of port around, and once they hit the shrapnel-churned fields of France, they would've been practically brushing their teeth in vermouth. But then again, who knows? It could've been cooked up by a Lithuanian umbrella-repairer in a coal cellar-turned-speakeasy in Union City, New Jersey.

Whoever formulated it, the Chancellor remains a dry and slightly mysterious little fiddle—not unlike a **Perfect Manhattan**, with port for the sweet vermouth and Scotch for the rye—that screams out 'club chair', 'billiards' and 'smoking jacket.' Point of advice: don't order it in an Irish bar. Or any bar, for that matter—better to err on the side of caution.

CHANCELLOR

Stir well with cracked ice:

2 oz Scotch whisky (blended, please)

1 oz ruby port

½ oz French vermouth

2 dashes orange bitters

Strain into chilled cocktail glass; it should pour a luminous garnet red.

CLIQUET

Pour in large Old-Fashioned glass:

1½ oz rye (*Esquire's* 1949 *Handbook for Hosts* suggests bourbon, which will also work)

Juice of 1 smallish orange

1 teaspoon dark Jamaica rum

Add 2 to 3 ice cubes and mix.

CLIQUET

The Web may be a wonderful thing, but nowhere on it will you find the origin of this drink. One search engine gives 3100 hits for 'cliquet'—which in French means 'clicky thing' or ratchet—and not a blessed one of 'em has anything to do with bourbon and orange juice. Nor do the standard bar books provide much enlightenment—all they tell us is that the bar at the old Waldorf-Astoria hotel (where the Empire State Building now stands) used to serve these, back in the rosy days before doing so became a criminal act. Not much, but it will suffice, for anything good enough for the patrons of 'the Hyphen' (as the W.-A. used to be known) is worth a second look.

But even assessed on its own merits, the Cliquet can pass muster. While not the kind of thing we'd serve in the evening, it does find a comfortable niche among the brunch drinks. It's simple, tasty, mellow and good for you (sort of—plenty of Vitamin C, anyway). And it doesn't involve vodka or tomato juice. There are people, it turns out, who don't care for vodka or tomato juice. Or celery, for that matter. And some of them like whiskey.

We like whiskey.

EMERALD

As we've observed elsewhere (see the **Brainstorm**), there aren't many Irish whiskey drinks on the books. What's more, most of the few you do find are stupid attempts at green beer, everybody's-Irish-on-St. Paddy's Day blarney (from our scorn we except, of course, the oft-abused but thoroughly divine **Irish Coffee**). No matter how dewy-eyed for the misty glens and chimney-snugs of the Auld Sod, we shall not be persuaded to sample the portable bog of Irish whiskey, green crème de menthe and green Chartreuse variously known as the **Erin's** or **Everybody's Irish**, the **Shamrock**, or the **Friendly Sons of St Patrick** (four cute names, one vile drink), and especially not when it is garnished, for good measure, with a green olive. Feh!

No, the only mixed drink with which we'll repeatedly toast the Emerald Isle is the Emerald. There's not much imagination in it, sure, its logic being, "if you mix rye, which they drink in New York, with vermouth, you get a **Manhattan**; therefore, Irish whiskey and vermouth must be an Emerald." But it's delightfully smooth and mellow. And if the reasoning's a little screwy, at least the only thing green about the drink is its title.

In fact, the Emerald presents rather an ethical dilemma: like the original **Manhattan**, it contains a dash of—oops—*orange* bitters. But maybe that's just to remind the sons of Erin that they shouldn't rest until the Saxon yoke is lifted from their fair and blooming isle and all true blood, bone and beauty can flourish in an air of tranquil peace and liberty. Or maybe someone just wasn't thinking. In either case, if your principles won't allow you to cross your lips with orange, you can leave the bitters out for an **Angelo-and-Mike**, or switch to Angostura bitters for a **Blarney Stone**. Or you can leave them in, but down your potion with a lusty, "To our enemies—may they be drinking bog water while we're drinking whiskey! May their obituaries be written in weasel's piss! May they shit sideways! May the hairs on their asses turn to drumsticks and beat them down to hell!" That's what we do, anyway (truth be told, the orange bitters make the drink).

EMERALD

Stir well with cracked ice:

2 oz Irish whiskey

1 oz Italian vermouth

Dash of orange bitters

Strain into chilled cocktail glass.

ESQUIRE

Shake well with cracked ice:

2¼ oz bourbon (preferably 100-
or 101-proof)

¾ oz Grand Marnier

1½ teaspoons fresh-squeezed
orange juice

1 teaspoon fresh-squeezed lemon
juice

1 or 2 dashes of Angostura
bitters (optional, but highly
recommended)

Strain into a chilled cocktail
glass and garnish
with a curl of
lemon rind.

ESQUIRE

'Esquire.' What a great name for a cocktail, right? Better than 'T.V. Guide' or 'Investor's Weekly', anyway (although perhaps not quite so good as 'Christian Science Monitor'). And yet, here in this great nation of America, you cannot stroll into your local shebeen and order an Esquire. Now, that's not for want of effort on our part—we've floated a couple of formulae, over the years. No go. Sank without a trace. Problem is, we trusted the experts to design 'em, or at least whomever we had on staff in charge of potables. Here's the kind of work they turned out: three parts dry vermouth, one part gin, straight up with a twist. Really.

Now, we thought we'd try again. This time, though, we figured we'd throw it open to the general public, make it a contest. The results couldn't be any worse, could they? Silly us. Setting aside all the berry- thises and banana- thats (we just don't drink that sort of thing), the 200-odd entries we received contained an awful lot of "pour 2 oz of Southern Comfort into a highball glass full of ice; top off with Fresca." Now, it's deplorable magazine etiquette to bust on the readership, but—no. And that's not even the worst of it. Here someone's polluting 20-year-old Glenlivet with Canadian whisky and cranberry juice, there it's Jack Daniel's getting the treatment, with cinnamon schnapps, triple sec and champagne. A certain "Chris G." captured the general tenor of things when he labeled his concoction "best when pantless."

Gradually, however, our faith in *Esquire* readers was vindicated: by the end of the contest, we had a good 25 drinks we could respect. How to choose? Bold and interesting, or classic and conservative? We tried a couple of the bold ones. "Fucking terrible." That's our editor, and we're not saying he's wrong. An Esquire should be something elegant, yet broad-shouldered; something that tastes good—very good—but doesn't go around shouting "Hey, lookit me!" Something, in short, that you'd drink more than once. (And strong.) Phil Broadhead, of Jackson, Mississippi, sent in this fine variation on the classic **Ward Eight**, which struck us all as being just the ticket.

By unanimous acclaim, we present the Esquire.

JUNIOR

If cocktails were buildings (and, Lord knows, that would explain some of the mixtures we've been subjected to of late), the Junior would be one of those sturdy old limestone loft buildings that line the side-streets of the typical downtown business district: not particularly flashy, but for all that possessed of good lines, hand-carved windows, a sculpted frieze, brass fittings. The very kind, unfortunately, that's too reticent in its charms to earn landmark status, and therefore is fated to crumble before the wrecking ball, only to be replaced by a prefab sour-apple schnapps-and-melon-liqueur office block, all sharp corners and flat, featureless planes.

Not if we can help it. The Junior, also known as the **Quick Recovery** (we can't explain either name, although the latter suggests it seeped up from the underworld of hangover cures), is eminently worth saving: the citrus frees the herbal notes of the Bénédictine from its heavy, sweet body, and both together buffer the tangy woodiness of the rye. Here's to landmark preservation!

ORIENTAL

The original **Savoy Cocktail Book** surrounds this suave muscle relaxant with a charming load of hooey having to do with a Dr. B— receiving this recipe in return for saving the life of "an American Engineer" in the Philippines, back in 1924. Well, maybe—but we'd bet even money that it was first formulated at the bar of, say, Broadway's old Oriental Hotel, or the one in Coney Island (or, for that matter, the one in Bangkok, which is still going strong). There's no way of checking, thank God, so here's to Dr. B—.

VARIANTS & MIXOLOGY

Cut the rye and paste in 1½ oz Scotch, ratchet the vermouth back half an ounce, and **Tom Johnstone** is in the house. Mr. J (1881–1965) was the man who brought electricity to the Scottish Highlands. With this?

JUNIOR

Shake well with cracked ice:

2 oz rye whiskey

½ oz lime juice

½ oz Bénédictine

Dash of bitters

Strain into chilled cocktail glass.

ORIENTAL

Shake well with cracked ice:

2 oz rye whiskey

½ oz Cointreau

1 oz Italian vermouth

½ oz lime juice

Strain into chilled cocktail glass.

ROB ROY

Stir well with cracked ice:

2 oz Scotch whisky (blended, please)

¾ oz Italian Vermouth

Dash of Angostura bitters (both *The Old Waldorf-Astoria Bar Book* and *The Stork Club Bar Book*—authorities of worth and probity—suggest orange bitters; listen to them)

Strain into chilled cocktail glass and garnish as you would a **Manhattan**, with a twist of lemon or, if you must, a cherry.

VARIANTS & MIXOLOGY

For the inevitable variation, there's the **Borden Chase** (Mr. Chase wrote hard-bitten fiction and, to his eternal credit, the screenplay for Howard Hawks' *Red River*): 2 oz blended Scotch, ¾ oz Italian vermouth, a dash of orange bitters, a dash of absinthe (or legal substitute); garnish with a twist of lemon.

Having finished that, you may move on to the **Glasgow**, assembling 1½ oz blended Scotch, 1½ oz French vermouth, 3 dashes absinthe (or…) and 3 dashes Angostura bitters, in the usual way.

ROB ROY

Henry Louis Reginald De Koven was born on April 3, 1859, in Middletown, Connecticut. He then proceeded to do a bunch of other stuff that culminated in his writing a sheaf of operettas for the national stage. Twenty-nine, by our count. Now, Reginald De Koven's music seemed to have a certain quality of *déjà entendu* which, while not necessarily posing a handicap when it came to drilling his melodies through the wax-plugged earholes of the shirtwaisted and mustachioed masses, did tend to excite a certain amount of comment in the profession, thus:

Enter VAUDEVILLE COMEDIAN, whistling tune.

VAUDEVILLE STRAIGHT MAN: "Isn't that De Koven's?"

V.C.: "Not yet!"

Applause, etc.

It didn't help matters that his two most successful shows (and they were pretty damn successful, we should add) were "Robin Hood"—"robbin' Ludwig," as they called it—from 1890 and, of course, 1894's "Rob Roy." Hence the drink.

It used to be a common practice to baptize a new show with its own cocktail (what'll it be? a Sexual Perversion in Chicago or a Miss Saigon—or a Little Mermaid on Ice?). Thus such forgotten delights as the Chocolate Soldier, the **Peg O' My Heart**, the **Florodora**. All decent drinks, but none with the legs of the Rob Roy. We attribute this to the occult correspondence that exists between the drink and the show: like De Koven's music, you see, there is a touch of the cut-and-paste to the Rob Roy. It's simply a **Manhattan** with the rye replaced by Scotch (Rob Roy being a Scottish national hero of some sort—not the one who daubed his buttocks blue and waved them at the English). Yet the result isn't bad. Perhaps a little odd, but in the long run quite rewarding. And they can make it in joints that know rye only as a vehicle for ham and Swiss cheese.

I'd say the drink has outlasted the music, but—"O Promise Me," that thing your ears tend to stumble into at certain kinds of wedding? De Koven's.

One of the greats. A New Orleans riff on the **Old-Fashioned** (or, as is more likely, on the **Old-Fashioned**'s progenitor, the original 'Cock-Tail'—this one's really old), the Sazerac is the kind of thing you'd put away a three-bagger of while sitting in some palooka dive two blocks down Eighth Avenue from Stillman's gym with your pal who works for *The Sporting News*, cracking peanuts and dissecting Cassius Clay's chances against Sonny Liston. A man's drink (although we've known plenty of dames who'd take one of these every time over some of the bellywash we see men drinking these days).

▲ **You can be sure Liston got more than this for the dive he took.**

SAZERAC

In an Old-Fashioned glass, muddle a sugar cube with a few drops of water. Add several small ice cubes and:

2½ oz rye whiskey—use the good stuff, if you can find it

3 drops Peychaud's bitters

Dash of Angostura bitters

Stir well and strain into a second, chilled, Old-Fashioned glass in which you have rolled around a few drops of absinthe (no substitute really works, but you can try a mix of Pernod and green Chartreuse) until its inside is thoroughly coated, pouring off the excess

Garnish with a twist of lemon peel.

Note: If we can't get the traditional rye, we'll have our Sazerac with brandy rather than use bourbon. But that's nothing new: the drink takes its name from Sazerac et Fils cognac, with which it was first made back in the uneasy days before the Civil War. See Last Call on page 188 on how to order Peychaud's bitters.

SUBURBAN

Stir well with cracked ice:

1½ oz rye whiskey

½ oz dark Jamaican rum

½ oz port

Dash of orange bitters

Dash of Angostura bitters

Strain into chilled cocktail glass.

SUBURBAN

The Suburban is a classic dark horse—you've never heard of it, you happen to take a flyer on it, and suddenly a string of famous names are eating its dust and there it is in the winner's circle. Its pedigree, however, is neither obscure nor undistinguished: according to *The Old Waldorf-Astoria Bar Book*, it was one of the drinks invented there to celebrate "the triumphs of James R. Keene and his racing cohorts and other famous stable-owners on near-by courses." Keene, who made his first pile off the legendary Comstock mine, was a Wall Street player whose fortunes were always fluctuating. Throughout his ups and downs, however, he maintained one of America's greatest stables—names like Commando, Colin and Sysonby are inscribed deep in the history of the turf. Keene's horses were fixtures in the Suburban Handicap, first run at Brooklyn's Sheepshead Bay track in 1884.

But enough about history. Let's talk mixology. If you could distill carved oak paneling and club chairs, leather-bound volumes and three-cushion billiard tables, this is what you'd get. Mellow, robust, comfortable. The rum mellows the tang of the rye, the port tames the alcohol, and the bitters add a touch of the exotic, like the stuffed head of that rare Asian gazelle which hangs over the doorway. Not a summer drink, but by August 15, we're willing to call it fall if it means we can have our Suburbans again.

Rye, by a nose, with rum to place and port to show. ▼

WARD EIGHT

In 1934, we voted this one of the ten best cocktails of the year. We're still trying to figure out why. Don't get us wrong: the Ward Eight's a perfectly delightful libation, dry and refreshing. But: A) it goes back to 1898, so hardly a new up-and-comer, and B) it's not a drink to change your views on life, happiness and the eternal mysteries with a single sip. Its aims are modest, its charms subtle. That is, if you make it right.

Tot homines, quot sententiae, the Romans used to say—so many people, that many opinions. Never has this been better illustrated than with the Ward Eight. Every authority, a different formula. Hell, things got so confusing the drinks correspondent for the old *New York Sun* (now there's a job) was driven to put the question to his readers; he got 400 answers. Some help.

Yet one thing stands certain: a proper Ward Eight must be based on rye, and it must contain orange juice. (If made with bourbon and only the lemon juice, as many suggest, it's just a **Whiskey Sour** with grenadine: a decent drink, but no Ward Eight.) Y'see, the sharp tang of the rye blends just so with the bite of the lemon and the rounded sweetness of the orange, leaving absolutely no taste of liquor. In short, this drink lies like a politician.

Which brings us to the name: they say this old smoothie was inaugurated at Boston's ancient Locke-Ober restaurant, at the victory supper (the night *before* the election, naturally) for Martin 'The Mahatma' Lomasney, running for something or other from Boston's Ward Eight—then located, as a reader informs us, "in the old West End…between Beacon Hill and the North End." We'd like to know how many Ward Eights they're pouring these days on Lomasney Way (yep—named a street after him).

WARD EIGHT

Shake well with cracked ice:

2 oz rye whiskey

¾ oz lemon juice

¾ oz fresh-squeezed orange juice

Scant teaspoon grenadine

Strain into chilled cocktail glass.

VARIANTS & MIXOLOGY

The Ward Eight is one of the older and better variations on the ol' **Whiskey Sour** (for one of the newer and better, see the **Esquire**). There are others, some decent, stretching from coast to coast—from the **Frisco** (3 oz bourbon, 1 oz Bénédictine, ½ oz lemon juice) to the **New Yorker** (2 oz rye, ½ oz lime juice, 1 teaspoon grenadine, with the option of pitching in half an egg-white). The Ward Eight also makes a fine cooler: simply strain into a Collins glass half-full of cracked ice and top up to taste with club soda or seltzer.

WHISKEY SOUR

Shake well with cracked ice:

2 oz bourbon or rye (or Canadian or Irish or…)

⅔ oz lemon juice (more or less, the juice of ½ decent-sized lemon)

1 teaspoon bar sugar

Strain into chilled cocktail glass (unless you happen to have the traditional Delmonico glass—a narrow-mouthed, slant-sided 6-oz tumbler). Resist, if you can, the impulse to decorate lavishly with fruit, although a maraschino cherry will raise no eyebrows.

WHISKEY SOUR

The Whiskey Sour is the fried-egg sandwich of American mixology: simple, dull, reliable in a pinch. It's nourishing, all right, but not a drink for cocktail time, for that hour of luminous blue when the more decorative and flush sectors of civilization exchange witticisms over icy glasses of invigorating drink. Uh-uh. Then, you want gin, vermouth or some combination of the two. Or, of course, a **Manhattan**. Something dressy. This? The cocktail in its undershirt.

And yet. At least since Stanley Kowalski, the ol' 'wife-beater', as the undershirt has so aptly become known, has had a certain rough sex appeal. If drinks were women—you want metaphors? we've got cases of 'em—the Whiskey Sour would be the over-the-hill blonde, all flesh and dishevelment, voice a half-drunken purr and eyes that tell you she ain't done yet. The drink has a peculiar seedy glory all its own. If you're embarked on that voyage to the end of the night, hurtling headlong to precincts where a tuxedo has never been seen, you'll want a pitcher of these at your side.

A couple words about the construction of this tipple: Sour mix? No. Whiskey? Whatever, as long as it's cheap. As in most whiskey drinks, we like rye—its tanginess ensures that it'll mix well without losing its identity—but bourbon works just fine. So does Irish whiskey. Canadian's okay, too. We've even heard of Scotch Sours, although never actually witnessed one passing the lips of a living human being. For that matter, you can use rum, or brandy, or even, should you find yourself on the back of the world, *arza*—you know, the stuff Central Asian nomads distill from fermented mare's milk? But in that case, you'll want to drink it hot, because cold it gives off an…aroma, let's just say.

VARIANTS & MIXOLOGY

For a change, try a **Dizzy Sour** (nothing to do with the trumpet-wrangler; the recipe's far more ancient than that): dock the whiskey ½ oz, add 3 dashes of Bénédictine and float ½ oz of dark Jamaica rum on top; garnish with a stick of pineapple, or not. You can also commit **Hari Kari**, our 1912 *Wehman Bros. Bartenders Guide* informs us, by building the standard recipe in a tall glass, topping it off with fizz water and bunging in whatever fruits you have in your garnish tray. If your poison's rum, we suggest substituting lime juice for the lemon (in which case you'll have a **Daiquiri**, but if you don't tell anyone we won't), and floating on a lid of 151–proof Demerara rum. And there's absolutely no need to resist the impulse to decorate lavishly. If, however, your poison's brandy, you might want to rein in the fruit salad—an orange slice and maybe the ol' cherry will be adequate—and point things up with a couple dashes of Angostura.

RUM COCKTAILS

BATISTE

No idea. It just shows up in our 1949 *Handbook for Hosts*, unencumbered by any sort of past whatsoever, like a naked amnesiac. Friendly little bugger, though. And easy on the eye.

RULE #45

If the bar doesn't carry it, don't fuss.

BATISTE

Stir well with cracked ice:

2 oz white rum

1 oz Grand Marnier

Strain into chilled cocktail glass; add the juice of half a lime and a twist of lemon peel and you have a **Prince George**.

CAIPIRINHA

Slice ½ lime into half-inch rounds, cube them, and muddle them in an Old-Fashioned glass or small tumbler with ½ teaspoon of bar sugar

Add a couple of ice cubes

Pour in 2 oz cachaça—Pitù is a common and acceptable brand

Serve with stirring rod.

CAIPIRINHA

The **Daiquiri's** Brazilian cousin, the Caipirinha might have been invented merely to serve as a perfect example of the compound French adjective, *jolie-laide*—literally, 'pretty-ugly.' Like the cheekbony, slash-mouthed model, this drink both repels and compels. Cachaça, the raw sugarcane spirit (in other words, rum) from which it is made, looks like vodka and tastes like it was aged in old truck tires. Yet, mixed with lime, sugar and ice, it intoxicates strangely and doesn't taste half bad.

◄ **(Watch those Caipirinhas, or you'll have trouble getting the straw into the coconut.)**

EL PRESIDENTE

The Floridita wasn't the only bar in Havana and Constantino Ribalaigua (see the **Daiquiri**) wasn't the only *coctelero*. Once the Volstead Act—the legal fiddle that put teeth into Prohibition—took hold in 1920, a lot of American bartenders decamped for points south (a priceless film exists of one of 'em, down in Havana, showing the camera how to build a **Daiquiri**, a word he can barely pronounce). Eddie Woelke, at Havana's Jockey Club, invented this one in honor of Gerardo Machado, the ex-cattle thief who ruled Cuba from 1925 to 1933.

This was a pretty popular drink, at one time. For instance, it was the house cocktail at the hot Club El Chico in Greenwich Village, where America was introduced to the rumba, in 1925; regulars considered the El Presidente "elixir for jaded gullets," according to the 1949 *Esquire's Handbook for Hosts*, and who are we to disagree. Here's how El Chico's bartender George Stadelman used to make 'em.

EL PRESIDENTE

Stir well with cracked ice:

1½ oz white or light-bodied golden rum (Puerto Rican or, of course, Cuban)

½ oz orange curaçao

¾ oz French vermouth

Dash of grenadine

Strain into chilled cocktail glass (it should pour a delightfully clear, deep orange color); garnish with a twist of orange peel.

HARPO'S SPECIAL

Shake well with cracked ice:

2 oz white rum

½ teaspoon curaçao

Juice of ½ lemon (lime works better)

½ teaspoon bar sugar

Drop of Angostura bitters

Strain into chilled cocktail glass.

Interestingly enough, should you alter this formula by substituting brandy for the rum and doubling the sugar, *mira!* It's El Floridita's **Brandy Cocktail Number I**, collected by Pemberton in February of that same year. Of course, for strict historical accuracy, you should strain this into a small, chilled Collins glass and garnish it with "a whole lemon peel, cut in a spiral and arranged thus inside the glass, and sprig of mint." It's still a good drink if you don't.

HARPO'S SPECIAL

The Harpo? Harpo Marx? Sure. Y'see, Murdock Pemberton, who managed our "Potables" column in the late 1930s, was a man of many parts, among them writing for the famous *Emporia Gazette*, criticizing art for *The New Yorker* and founding the legendary Algonquin Round Table. One day in 1919, he, critic Alexander Woolcott and some other guy had lunch at the Algonquin (see the **Algonquin**) and decided to do it again the next day. The lunch date lasted twelve years. People came, people went, among them Dorothy Parker, Robert Benchley, George S. Kaufman—and Harpo Marx.

Pemberton printed this elegant variation on the **Daiquiri** in June, 1939.

HOTEL NACIONAL SPECIAL

Yet another episode from Cuba's never-ending struggle for freedom (see the **Daiquiri** and the **Cuba Libre**). October 2, 1933: after six months of wild political rugby that saw the fall of one strongman, General Gerardo Machado (see the **El Presidente**), and the rise of another, Sergeant—now Colonel—Fulgencio Batista, along with a whole lot of other foofaraw far too complicated to get into in a drink essay, it's come to this: 300 army officers are holed up in Cuba's best hotel, the Nacional (549 rooms, each with bath), surrounded by Batista's troops. Will P. Taylor, the Hotel's American manager (and former manager of the old Waldorf-Astoria), has been convinced to assist his guests to the full extent of his capacity. Does that include providing unlimited refills of this, his pet creation? History is silent.

If the officers *had* been raising their morale with these, though, they would've had the last of them to be poured for quite some time: the day ended with the hotel being heavily shelled, the officers' surrender (after losing twenty or so men), and the looting of the hotel's cellars. The hotel, at least, was insured (it's still there). The drink, by the way, is excellent.

◀ **The Nacional, still going strong. Ask for a no-shelling floor.**

HOTEL NACIONAL SPECIAL

Stir well with cracked ice:

2 oz golden Puerto Rican or Cuban rum

1½ oz unsweetened pineapple juice

½ oz lime juice

1 teaspoon dry (Hungarian) apricot brandy

Strain into chilled cocktail glass.

This, as globetrotting mixologist Charles Baker notes, is closely related to another Cuban drink, the **Mary Pickford** (movie stars liked to drink just like everybody else—maybe more; at any rate, Pickford received the honor of a drink—2 oz white rum, 1 oz unsweetened pineapple juice, 2 teaspoon grenadine—by the great Eddie Woelke, bartender at Havana's Jockey Club).

PRESIDENTE VINCENT

Shake well with cracked ice:

2 oz Haitian rum (Barbancourt is
a good brand; if you can't find
that, you can substitute a rhum
from Martinique or even a
golden Puerto Rican rum—Ron
del Barrilito works well)

1 oz French vermouth

1 oz lime juice (juice of 1 lime)

1 teaspoon bar sugar

Strain into chilled cocktail glass
that has had its rim rubbed with
lime juice and dipped in sugar.

PRESIDENTE VINCENT

It should probably be 'President Vincent', with no 'e' and pronounced 'Pray-zee-DAHNT:' Sténio Vincent was the guy in charge of Haiti when the Yankees were persuaded to clear off after nineteen years of the U.S.M.C. running all over the place and getting in everyone's hair. That was back in 1934. We suspect his patronage of the cocktail is merely in name, but short of reading thick books in foreign languages, we'll never know. And as long as a ready supply of these lovelies is at hand, the chances of that happening are pretty near nil.

We do like to visualize—based on no evidence whatsoever—*Monsieur le Président* standing on the dock with a pitcher of these when F.D.R., out cruising the Caribbean for some reason or other, stopped in Haiti to iron out the final details for extracting the gyrenes. Since, whenever at home, Roosevelt insisted on making his own drinks, and since he was a notoriously incompetent mixologist, it would've been one of the few times he got something civilized under his belt.

But the name of the drink as it comes down to us is 'Presidente Vincent', with the honorific spelled the Spanish way. This makes us suspect that this variant on the **El Presidente** should actually be notched up to the corps of genius bartenders for which Cuba used to be famous, no doubt toasting their neighbor's success at Yanqui-wrangling. However you spell it, whoever devised it, this is one of the best warm-weather drinks going, dry and refreshing yet still mellow and flavorful. Which reminds us—*garçon*!

VARIANTS & MIXOLOGY

There is a variant, the **Roosevelt** (naturally), in which you replace the lime juice with half as much orange juice (the Prez was famously partial to the **Orange Blossom**, which in his rendition supposedly caused Winston Churchill to refuse a second drink—as unlikely as that may seem).

SUNSHINE

Most old drinks books list a Sunshine Cocktail, and they're all different. Gin, rum, crème de cassis, sweet vermouth, dry vermouth, lemon juice, lime juice, pineapple juice, orange wine (made only in Florida, from rotten oranges—really), orange bitters, Angostura bitters… Where does it end?

Careful and patient study enables the drink taxonomist to assign the bulk of these specimens into three main phyla: one is simply a sweet **Martini**, not unlike the **Hearst**. The other two share the combination of white rum and French vermouth but diverge sharply after that, one into the world of fancy Continental liqueurs (shake with cracked ice a half-tablespoon each of crème de cassis and lemon juice and an ounce and a half each of white rum and French vermouth; strain and serve). Fine, if you like that sort of thing.

The other, well, it goes into advertising. Now, 'sunshine' being synonymous in the popular imagination with 'Florida', and Florida producing a lot of pineapple juice (which the drink contains), one might suppose that some functionary for the South Florida Pineapple Board—or a Madison Avenue Martini-sump in his employ—edited the old Sunshine into his marketing plan by simply cutting the cassis and lemon and pasting in good old Florida pineapple juice, with a splash of grenadine so the color comes out right. Close. The true origins of this suave pick-me-up seem to lie a bit farther to the south: it first turns up in the 1930s, in a little promo booklet the folks at Bacardi published in Santiago de Cuba, where they had their HQ. (And where, one should note, the man who would eventually expropriate their operation was an as-yet beardless schoolboy). But not everything of commercial origin is bad, as Captain Crunch and the career of Clint Eastwood demonstrate, so sip away with head held high and pleasure undiminished by doubt.

SUNSHINE

Shake well with cracked ice:

2 oz white rum

½ oz French vermouth

¾ oz pineapple juice

Dash of grenadine

Strain into chilled cocktail glass.

If you want to add a dash of Peychaud's bitters, should you have such a thing, it'll add a certain edge to the drink that is not unpleasing.

VERA RUSH

Pour in Old-Fashioned glass, with lump of ice:

2 oz dark Jamaican rum (if you can't get Myers's, Gosling's Bermuda will do nicely)

Float ½ oz unsweetened pineapple juice on top.

VERA RUSH

Let us pause for a moment to contemplate the bounty of on-premises beverage alcohol retailers—all right, bars—with which a benevolent creation has endowed this vast nation. Yet in the gleaming **Cosmopolitan**-mill of the urban bourgeoisie, all brushed aluminum and woods you can't find at Home Depot, no less than in the backcountry beer-bunker, sunk deep in its unswept, nicotine-blackened gloom, nine out of ten times—ninety-five out of a hundred—you won't be able to get a decent cocktail (the **Martini** generally, but by no means always, excepted). You ask for a **Sidecar**, hardly the Manhattan Project of mixology, and you get about a half-pint of lukewarm Cointreau diluted with citric acid and topped up with, we dunno, white rum? Midori? In many—most—of these joints, they'll even find ways to screw up a vodka drink, something traditional mixology holds to be an impossibility. And yet we have seen it. What to do?

You can cave and have a **Martini**, if that's an option (sometimes it's not—enough said). Or you can fight the good fight, lecture and educate. Or, if you'd rather not look like an asshole, you can have one of these simple charmers. Order it thus, as silent-film queen Vera Rush (*Intemperance, The Graven Image*) used to: "Myers's on the rocks with a splash of pineapple juice." Infallible, and always in style.

BRANDY COCKTAILS

BRANDY DAISY

The Daisy is one of the older drinks in the mixologist's cupboard, dating from the mid-nineteenth century, an especially fertile time in the history of the art. When Americans weren't busy chasing each other back and forth across the countryside in uniformed mobs, it seems, they were cogitating new compounds to throw a lip over. The basic construction of the Daisy involves firewater—any firewater—with lemon juice and some kind of liquid sweetener, alcoholic or non, the whole mess being served on ice in a stemmed glass and decorated like an Easter-bonnet. The varieties were legion.

But it's the new millennium, and we're not in the habit of drinking antiques. When was the last time you had a Sherry Cobbler? A Port Wine Flip? A Brandy Champarelle? Hell, even old **Tom Collins** seems to be declining to a dusty death, and there's no nobler drink in creation. So why pull this one out of the closet? The way it's usually presented—brandy, lemon juice, grenadine, sugar, poured over crushed ice and topped off with fizz water and fruit—there's really no reason. Pleasant, but dull.

Yet, as so often happens, the past we're presented with is considerably less interesting and complex than the past as it was actually lived. The Brandy Daisy recipe offered by Professor Jerry Thomas (see the **Tom and Jerry**) is far more alluring, calling as it does for curaçao instead of the usually-insipid grenadine and accenting the whole with a couple dashes of fragrant Jamaica rum (brandy's closest friend in the spirit world). Yummy.

Even better, however, is the maverick formula transmitted by one Edward Spencer Mott, an Englishman who sometimes scribbled under the name of 'Nathaniel Gubbins'—not to be confused with Bartholomew Cubbins—in 1899: the Chartreuse's herbal notes float lightly above the fullness of the brandy, while the lemon juice cuts the heaviness of the liqueur. Antiquing can be fun; who knew?

BRANDY DAISY

Shake well with cracked ice:

2 oz brandy

1 oz yellow Chartreuse

1 oz lemon juice

Strain into chilled cocktail glass.

Mott calls for sugar, which is unnecessary. To bring this more in line with Daisy orthodoxy, half-fill a silver julep mug or stemmed wine-goblet with cracked ice, pour in the ingredients, top 'em off with a couple ounces of seltzer or club soda, and stir until the glass frosts. Decorate with sprig of mint and wheels of orange and lemon and harpoon with straw.

BETWEEN THE SHEETS

Shake well with cracked ice:

1½ oz cognac or other French brandy (although a Spanish brandy rounds off some of the drink's edge)

1½ oz Puerto Rican gold-label rum (white rum is traditional, but, as Embury points out, the gold combines better with brandy)

½ oz Cointreau

1 oz lemon juice (Embury suggests lime, but lemon is traditional)

Strain into chilled cocktail glass and garnish with a twist of lemon.

RULE #234

Never order a drink named after a sex act.

BETWEEN THE SHEETS

The ancestor of all the Silk Panties, Slippery Nipples, Screaming Orgasms and Sloe Comfortable Screws that so titillate the Abercrombie & Fitch set, the Between the Sheets dates to Prohibition—when, frankly, the nation's moral fiber wasn't what it ought to have been. But then again, neither was the nation's liquor supply. Which led to perversions like this—smutty name, too much alcohol.

A bartender of the old—pre-Prohibition—school would have been leery of combining two main liquors like this (supposedly it would lead to "sudden intoxication," which with liquor going for dollars a drink was no bad thing, and "sick headaches afterwards," which would fall under the heading of acceptable risk). In fact, this is one of the drinks that O.B. (Original Bartender, of course) Patrick Gavin Duffy printed with an asterisk, indicating a cocktail he "personally [did] not recommend."

That said, the B.t.S. is a perfectly (or at least not-imperfectly) charming potion—stronger than its kissing cousin the **Sidecar** and almost as smooth, although without the **Sidecar's** peculiar magic. Our recipe is based on the one master mixologist David Embury offered in his *Fine Art of Mixing Drinks*, the only work in existence to address the theoretical aspects of the subject.

VARIANTS & MIXOLOGY

If your mood will not support the Between the Sheets' lingering vulgarity, might we suggest the enigmatically-named but *très suave* **Three Miller**? It ratchets the hooch back a notch while preserving the intriguing rum-brandy combination; prepare as above, but up the brandy to two ounces, dock the rum by half an ounce and replace the Cointreau with a scant teaspoon of grenadine. A Duffy recipe, printed without asterisk (it seems that mixing two liquors is kosher if one of them is just used as an accent).

METROPOLE

If drinks were old movie stars, this one would be James Mason. Dark, handsome, suave, a little dry, but deep down a swine. Which is entirely appropriate, considering what it was named after.

The Hotel Metropole, right off Times Square, was not the kind of hotel to host Austrian Princes or, for that matter, delegations of Midwestern church-ladies. First of all, it was only six stories, and narrow. More important, it was, as Albert Stevens Crockett noted in *The Old Waldorf–Astoria Bar Book*, "somewhat lively." That's a euphemism. You see, the Café Metropole on the ground floor had an all-night license and a showy clientele studded with crooked ward-heelers, mid-level gamblers, palookas and their handlers, actors (you know how they are), and every other kind of half-hand bigshot who talks sideways and never looks you in the eye except when he's dealing from the bottom of the deck.

That was the Metropole. It went bankrupt in July, 1912, a week after witnessing the murder of one of its regulars, Beansy Rosenthal—for whom see the **Jack Rose**.

METROPOLE

Stir well with cracked ice:

1½ oz brandy (if a little plush-ness is desired, try a Spanish brandy such as Fundador)

1½ oz French vermouth

1 dash orange bitters

2 dashes Peychaud's bitters

Garnish with maraschino cherry. Without the cherry or the Peychaud's, if you pitch in a twist of lemon you've got a simple **Brandy Cocktail**.

SENSATION (ALIAS BRANDIED PORT)

Shake well with cracked ice:

2 oz decent ruby port

1 oz brandy (Spanish works particularly well)

Dash of fresh-squeezed orange juice (optional but delicious; Michael Johnson always added it, which is good enough for us)

Strain into chilled cocktail glass and garnish with twist of lemon peel (or, if you're using the O.J., orange peel).

VARIANTS & MIXOLOGY

Note: this Sensation is not to be confused with the one that combines 2 oz gin, ½ oz lemon juice and 1 teaspoon maraschino—properly, an **Aviation**—with mint. Coincidentally, some take their Brandied Port with those same quantities of maraschino and lemon juice (and no O.J.). And there is, of course, a **Churchill** cocktail: 1½ oz Scotch, ½ oz each Cointreau, Italian vermouth and lime juice, shaken and strained; we printed the formula in September, 1939, before Winnie took up the reins of state. There's also this **Churchill**, invented, so the 1965 *Esquire Party Book* says, by Sir Winston himself: gently stir 3 oz brandy, 1½ oz champagne and a dash of Cointreau with cracked ice and strain into a champagne flute. Dot-dot-dot-dash.

SENSATION (ALIAS BRANDIED PORT)

Reasonably enough, most winter drinks in the repertoire trace their origins to Northern Europe. It's cold in those parts, and the natives like alcohol. Problem is, their taste buds appear to be made of vulcanized asbestos. Ask anyone. Bashed neeps, lutefisk, toad-in-the-hole—the list of gastric crimes is long and violent. And, unfortunately, this talent for palate-assault has not left their mixology unmarked. Not always, thank God—**Irish Coffee**, for example, holds a place among the compounds benevolent to humankind somewhere in between penicillin and hemoglobin. Far more typical, however, are those boiled-wine-and-spice things that taste like liquid fruitcake—but since America has collectively weighed in on the subject of fruitcake (see the Christmas episode of any sitcom), there's no need for us to add to the abuse. Still, you have to drink *something*, and there are occasions where a straight shot of the naked creature won't do. That's when the Sensation springs to its sleigh, shouting "drink away! Drink away! Drink away all!"

We were first introduced to this liquid insulator some time in the late 1980s, at Manhattan's lamented Quatorze (the prototype of today's retro bistro). Whenever the thermometer got sluggish, waiter and boy-about-town Michael Johnson could always be counted on to whip up a batch to help the staff and their after-hours pals brave the chill winds of West Fourteenth St. But the drink is a good deal older than that.

Consider its components. Brandy. Port. Clearly, this drink could only have sprung from the fertile genius of Sir Winston Churchill—these two tipples being the principal fuels for his bulldog temper (plus, of course, liberal injections of Johnnie Walker, Pol Roger, Pouilly Fumé, etc, *ad libitum*). Would that we could confirm that origin. But we can't (the drink turns up without announcement in our June, 1939 "Potables" column). Still, what's the harm in pretending? So should you happen to come across us loitering in the vicinity of the winter solstice, just mix us up a pitcher of these and we'll be ready to fight 'em on the beaches.

SIDECAR

The Sidecar is often singled out as the only good cocktail to come out of the long national nightmare that was Prohibition. And when you're sipping one, you almost think it was all worth it. The luminous, golden-straw color, the perfectly controlled sweetness, the jazzy high notes of the citrus against the steady bass of the brandy. This is a drink whose suavité is beyond question—it's the Warren Beatty of modern mixology. It's so easy, in fact, to be seduced by this clever old roué that a word of caution would not be out of place here. These gents have a way of stealing up on you and bimmo! Next thing you know it's 8:43 on Monday morning and you're sitting in the back seat of a taxi idling in front of your place of employ. In your skivvies.

While unanimity prevails as to what goes into a Sidecar, there's considerable dissention about how much of each. The French school, as it's known, holds to a Trinitarian philosophy—three equal parts. It has some standing in this matter, as this stripped-down variation on the **Brandy Daisy** is supposed to have been invented in France, towards the end of World War I (in later editions of Scots-born, Paris-based barkeep Harry MacElhone's *Harry's ABC of Mixing Cocktails*—see the **White Lady**—he credits himself for it; in earlier ones, however, he names Pat McGarry of Buck's Club, London, inventor of the **Mimosa**; hmm). Be that as it may, we like more of the Holy Ghost in ours.

Was the Sidecar a British plant? ▶

SIDECAR

Shake well with cracked ice:

1 oz Cointreau

1 oz lemon juice

2 oz brandy (use a decent cognac)

Strain into chilled cocktail glass that has had its rim rubbed with lemon juice and dipped in sugar. Some claim good results replacing the brandy with golden Puerto Rican rum.

Esquire's 13 Best Drinks
(That Your Friends Have Never Heard of)

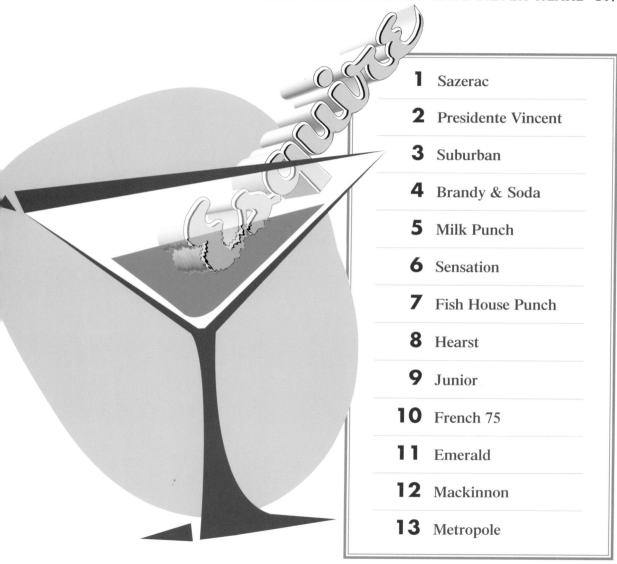

1	Sazerac
2	Presidente Vincent
3	Suburban
4	Brandy & Soda
5	Milk Punch
6	Sensation
7	Fish House Punch
8	Hearst
9	Junior
10	French 75
11	Emerald
12	Mackinnon
13	Metropole

OTHER HOOCHES

BLUE MONDAY

BLUE MONDAY

Stir well with cracked ice:

2 oz vodka

½ oz Cointreau

2 to 3 drops blue food coloring

Strain into chilled cocktail glass and, we suppose, drink.

This simple little device has the distinction of being the first documented silly vodka drink. First printed in the English *Savoy Cocktail Book* in 1930, the Blue Monday spices up vodka with a splash of Cointreau, which is just a superior brand of triple sec or white curaçao. So far, so good. But then it pitches in a drop or two of blue food coloring—yielding, of course, a blue drink, a color not found in the natural world of the mixed drink. Vodka is not blue, nor gin, nor of course whiskey, brandy, rum or any other liquor produced by the natural processes of distillation, aging and filtration.

The next step? Simple: premix the curaçao and the dye. When was blue curaçao introduced? We're not sure; we do know it was a European thing, like this drink, and it first seems to have reached these shores after World War II. Did the drink lead to the liqueur? Could be, as Bugs Bunny says. (To be honest, there were already two blue liqueurs on the market before this one, Crème Yvette, which was flavored with violets and hence came by its color more-or-less honestly, and Parfait Amour, which counts orange among its flavors and gets its color from chemistry and thus did not). But if we had to blame somebody for making the Windex Margarita possible, it would be the creator of the Blue Monday—inoffensive though it may be.

RULE #651

That blue cocktail you ordered will • • • • • • not impress.

COSMOPOLITAN

Shake well with cracked ice:

2 ounces vodka

1 oz Cointreau

1 oz cranberry juice

½ oz lime juice

Strain into chilled cocktail glass.

Some use Rose's instead of the fresh-squeezed lime juice; to complain about this, whether because the stuff's kinda artificial tasting or because it makes the drink too sweet, strikes us as taking the Cosmo way too seriously (if you didn't like sweet drinks, you wouldn't have ordered a Cosmo in the first place, and since the cranberry juice comes from sweetened concentrate, why not the lime?). Some frost the rim of the glass with sugar, à la **Sidecar**; it looks great—the Cosmopolitan's strong point—so why not. Some even suggest a dash of orange bitters, if you can get them.
It couldn't hurt.

COSMOPOLITAN

"**Juice Boxes for yuppies**" —NICK NOYES

A mutant child of the **Sidecar** and the **Cape Codder**, the Cosmopolitan was the theme drink of the 1990s: like Celebration, Florida—the Disney town—it has all the appearance of tradition without any of the workmanship. The purpose of a cocktail is to take the pronounced, even pungent, flavor of a liquor and, through careful blending with acids, aromatics and essences, transform it into something new and hitherto-untasted. But vodka has no flavor: if a cocktail is chemistry, this is just mixing.

RULE #57

A cocktail should not take you back to your childhood, unless of course you grew up in a bar.

DULCHIN

Subtle, potent and delightfully mysterious, the Dulchin was created—we're not sure exactly when—for a scion of the New York hardware dynasty of that name who was allergic to grain distillates and tired of rum. Stump your friends.

DULCHIN

Shake well with cracked ice:

2 oz pisco (see **Pisco Punch**)

1 oz dry (Hungarian) apricot brandy

2 teaspoons Grand Marnier

1 oz lime juice

1 teaspoon grenadine

Strain into chilled cocktail glass.

HOP TOAD

A slippery one, this, but worth catching if the effort required isn't too great (best case: somebody gives you a bottle of Hungarian apricot brandy). There's an unusual amount of variation among the old recipes, involving everything from the kind of brandy—some misguided souls say grape—to the name, with detours through Jamaica rum and apricot liqueur. Weighing all the evidence, though, the philosophy of the Hop Toad seems to be to allow the lime juice to fall tart on the tongue, without making the result so sour as to be undrinkable. To create, in other words, a state of dynamic tension by placing the drink in a condition of carefully calibrated imbalance. What that has to do with amphibians, we don't know.

To our taste, the recipe from Tom Bullock's 1917 *Ideal Bartender* (he called it the **Leaping Frog**) has the most snap to it.

HOP TOAD

Shake well with cracked ice:

2 oz dry (Hungarian) apricot brandy

⅔ oz lime juice

Strain into chilled cocktail glass.

JACK ROSE

Shake well with cracked ice:

2 oz applejack (the only domestic brand we've managed to turn up is still made in Jersey, by the Lairds; they've been making it since the 1600s)

Juice of 1 lime

Scant ½ oz grenadine

Strain into chilled cocktail glass.

RULE # 110

Squeeze those lemons, limes, oranges yourself— work is ennobling.

JACK ROSE

Jack Rose was a bald liar. In the early-morning hours of July 13, 1912, a mid-level gambler by the name of Herman 'Beansy' Rosenthal was called away from the 2 a.m. ginger ale he was sipping (actually, it was a **Horse's Neck**—ginger ale on the rocks with the spiral-cut peel of a lemon; one cannot be too precise in matters mixological) in the bar of Times Square's Hotel Metropole (see the **Metropole**) and shot four times in the head. Bald Jack Rose was the guy who handled the contract. Here's the liar part: when Herbert Bayard Swope of the *New York World* and D.A. Charlie Whitman got together—for reasons too complex to go into in a drink essay—to frame a certain Lieutenant Charles Becker of the NYPD's anti-gambling squad for ordering the hit, Rose was their star witness. Perjured himself with enthusiasm and imagination (and, of course, saved his neck). It was the "trial of the century;" little did they know. Becker went to the chair, Whitman to the Governor's office, Swope to the executive editorship of the *World* and Rose—well, he went into the catering business.

It's even remotely possible that Rose himself invented this drink; served it up to his customers: he was somewhat of a celebrity (whatever became of that Kaelin fellow, anyway?) and not averse to cashing in on his ill-gotten fame. But whoever it was, he was a clever bugger—the drink is based on apple-*jack*, and it's *rose*-pink. Play on words. In any case, the Jack Rose is an effective testament to its namesake: it's smooth and sweetish and deeply deceptive. Sipping it, you can't tell it contains liquor of any kind, let alone applejack. Ironic: the one classic cocktail still enjoying some currency to use New Jersey's indigenous firewater, and you can't taste it.

MARGARITA

A relative newcomer to cocktail Olympus, the Margarita is the last great cocktail to come into wide use before the vodka revolution sent the finer points of mixology to the guillotine. Although its roots are deep—the divine combination of tequila, lime juice and Cointreau first turns up in the 1937 *Café Royal Cocktail Book*, published in London (of all places), and the name seems to date from the 1940s—the Margarita is really a child of the 1970s. Most bar books before the 1960s don't even mention tequila (although, we note with pride, our 1955 *Esquire Drinks Book* was hip to the Margarita). And if by 1967, you find *The Booze Book*, a most groovy compendium, offering two tequila concoctions—neither is the Margarita. In 1973, however, the Margarita has arrived; *Esquire*'s revised *Handbook for Hosts* lists it among the "twelve most useful of all drinks."

Essentially a variation on the **Sidecar**—tequila for brandy, lime juice for lemon, salt rim for sugar—the Margarita shares its characteristic luminosity and, especially, its sneakiness. Yet it's a completely different drink, less plush than the Sidecar but more dignified (when properly made, of course—without strawberries and suchlike cargo).

TEQUILA SUNRISE

The 1970s. Ugh. Earth shoes. The AMC Pacer. The Maxi. Helen Reddy. And, of course, the Tequila Sunrise, a drink which, if it wasn't named after that Eagles song—when was that? 1973?—at least it got a great big whanging boost from it. Now, some claim the drink goes back to Tijuana in the 1920s, but really—no Eagles, no Tequila Sunrise. That's the higher truth. Mythology trumps mixology, just about every time. And, we have to concede, as stupid as this little gimmick may be in the larger sense (it's really not much of a drink, admit it), its consumption is not unattended by a feeling of easeful peace. Irony? The guy in the song was drinking his tequila in shots, not mixed with O.J. and grenadine. Decision? Contingent on level of nostalgia for the Ford years.

MARGARITA

Shake well with cracked ice:

2 oz good-quality silver tequila (it should be 100 percent agave—the plant from which the stuff is traditionally made; Herradura or Cuervo Tradicional yield excellent results. Save the great golden añejos for sipping)

1 oz Cointreau or triple sec (although definitely the posh alternative, Cointreau yields results demonstrably superior to triple sec, most brands of which have an unpleasant chemical aftertaste)

1 oz lime juice

Strain into chilled cocktail glass that has had its rim rubbed with lime juice and dipped in coarse salt.

TEQUILA SUNRISE

In the bottom of large, chilled cocktail glass, add 1½ teaspoons of grenadine and put aside

Shake well with cracked ice:

1½ oz tequila

3 oz fresh-squeezed orange juice

Strain into said cocktail glass

Stir only enough to produce the sunrise effect (you know, layers of oranges and reds and whatnot).

VODKA MARTINI

Our preferred ratio of vodka to vermouth is 18:1.

Shake well with cracked ice:

3 oz vodka (we like the Russian stuff in this; it's a bit chewier, with some traces of flavor)

1 teaspoon French vermouth

Strain into chilled cocktail glass and garnish with a twist (or an olive). Truth be told, we find the Kanga...the Vodka Martini much improved by a dash of orange bitters.

Winston Churchill gives vodka a backhanded endorsement (lovely stuff—if you've run out of brandy, port, champagne, gin and Scotch). ▼

VODKA MARTINI

The old, cynical star and the sweet young hopeful who seems happy just to be her doormat. We all know the story—they made a movie about it. *All About Eve*...won, like, six Academy Awards...1950...black-and-white...Bette Davis... "Fasten your seatbelts, it's going to be a bumpy night"...the doormat ends up with all the cake. That one.

Anyway, as things start off, the ingenue wouldn't dream of comparing herself to the star, not openly. So first, in 1934, it's only the **Vodka Cocktail** (Frank Shay wrote it up in the December *Esquire*). Generic name, no threat. But inspection of the recipe discloses that it's nothing more than a **Perfect Martini** (2 parts gin, 1 part mixed sweet and dry vermouth), but with vodka. Yet this could conceivably be construed as a version of the **Perfect Manhattan** (same, but with whiskey), so no real encroachment on the gin **Martini**'s position. Two years later, though, a New York restaurant's serving "practically a Martini, except vodka is used in lieu of gin." Serious cause for concern, but the drink's calling itself the **Russian Special**—still not a direct challenge. Then came the war.

Suddenly, Russia's our ally, vodka is chic—"if you wish to seem extra sophisticated, order vodka instead of cocktails," food- and sports-writer (nice combo, no?) Iles Brody advised in 1945—and the gin supply is shaky (all those exotic spices aren't exactly priority cargo). What to drink? The **V-Martini** (V for 'victory'/V for 'vodka': same-same). Now, vodka can make the case that it's just helping out when times are tough, but you know how that tends to turn out. The fashion-forward read the tea leaves and begin to switch: the 1946 *Stork Club Bar Book* has two recipes for the Vodka Martini, just like that.

It's around this time that whimsical mixologist Crosby Gaige prints the thing under the name **Kangaroo Cocktail**, which neatly sums up what's going on: the V. M.'s bouncing into cocktail glory in the gin **Martini's** pouch. (That name never really caught on; neither did the compromise **Vodkatini**, which settled for taking only half its rival's name.) Now, of course, vodka with vermouth is calling itself a **Martini**, without a prefix; such is the right of a conqueror. On the bright side, the Vodka Martini's icy, refreshing, and smooooth. What it isn't, however, is a **Martini**. Those you make with gin. We shall never surrender on that.

Enough Mojitos and *everyone* looks like this.

TALL DRINKS

NOT ALL DRINKING takes place between five and eight in the evening, with everybody dressed up nice. What about the long, lazy afternoon in the country? The outdoors café in the tropical port? The shady porch in bluegrass country? The occasions for thirst… there are just so many.

RULE #564

Never
have more
than three
cocktails.

After three
cocktails,
switch to
Highballs.

RULE #387

THE HIGHBALL

The invention of the highball, "high priest of tall drinks," as our 1949 *Handbook for Hosts* dubbed it, was claimed by Patrick Gavin Duffy, bartender at Manhattan's Ashland House (Fourth Avenue at Twenty-fourth Street, if you care).

That was back around 1890. Seeing as it's nothing but spirits—whiskey at first, then whatever—ice, and soda water or ginger ale (an early innovation), you'd think it wouldn't take much inventing, but before then no red-blooded American drinker would have conceived of introducing water, of all things, into good red whiskey, tiny bubbles or no. So they say, anyway. (There's also the question of Duffy's intimacy with the **Brandy and Soda**, which they were drinking in England in the early-nineteenth century, and the problem of what to do with the **Splificator**, the gloriously-named recipe for what sounds suspiciously like a highball, published by Chris Lawlor of the Burnet House, Cincinnati, in 1895.) But if the name's all that Duffy invented, that's plenty, in our book—even if nobody's precisely sure where he got it.

Simple as the Highball may be, it's not without principles:

1   Use a tall—at least 12 oz—narrow-mouthed glass (preserves the bubbles).

2   Put in the ice—2 or 3 cubes are plenty; some Brits prefer theirs without ice. Let 'em go it on their own hook.

3   Add your chosen liquor—the Highball began as a whiskey drink, but soon became less exclusive—over the ice. Don't slug it: it's better to have two pleasant belts than one knuckle-duster (although if the drink's potency is the result of a bartender's kindness, it would of course be churlish to kick about it). For normal use, two or three ounces should do nicely.

4   Pour in the sparkling water (club soda or seltzer). If at all possible, this should be refrigerated in order to keep the ice from melting prematurely and drowning the bubbles. How much? Less than equal the amount of hooch is too strong, more than three times too weak.

No need to stir—if the water's got any life left in it, the bubbles will take care of that. In any case, avoid stirring with metal, which is supposed to "squelch" the bubbles. "If one of your guests is stir-crazy," our 1949 *Handbook for Hosts* advises, "give him a plastic or glass swizzle stick." In any case, serve it up immediately.

The following half-dozen of the myriad possible sub-species of Highballs have taken on lives of their own.

HIGHBALLS

BRANDY AND SODA

Bertie Wooster—Jeeves's employer, for those not conversant with the doings of the Drones Club—may have possessed, as he readily admitted, about "half the amount of brain a normal bloke ought to possess," but he was no dummy when it came to getting outside something alcoholic. Formerly much-frequented, the old 'b. and s.' (east of Suez, they called it the '**Peg**', as in coffin-) was—along with the **Pink Gin**, which nobody drinks anymore either—one of the props that kept the British upper classes from tottering into oblivion, where for all intents and purposes they may now be found. There's a lesson in there somewhere.

However you pronounce your 'aitches', this is a fine, mellow alternative to the **Scotch and Soda**, not entirely free from affectation but well short of the cravat and the small, carefully-hedged mustache. (For some reason, the b. and s. is particularly topping when consumed on an airplane.)

BRANDY AND SODA

Pour 2 or 3 oz of brandy into a Collins glass holding 2 or 3 ice cubes and top up with soda. That's all there is to it. (Use a well-grade French brandy, one of the cheaper cognacs, or just about any Spanish brandy, but save the pricey stuff for your after-dinner snifter.)

VARIANTS & MIXOLOGY

For a **Burrah Peg**, double the amount of hooch, burrah meaning 'big' in Hindi; for a **Chota**—'little'—**Peg**, or **Stengah** (from the Malay *satengah*, 'one half'), pour it on the light side. Either of these potions can be made with Scotch, and frequently were (especially after the French rolled over back in 1940 and the brandy supply dried up). One that can't, or at least wasn't, is the **King's Peg**, which replaces the common soda water with chilled brut champagne (you can leave out the ice). We like these. A lot.

PRESBYTERIAN

Pour 2 oz blended Scotch into a Collins glass, add 2 or 3 ice cubes and top up with ginger ale, or half ginger ale and half club soda.

PRESBYTERIAN

"Scotch whisky and what? Nah. That's just plain weird, man. Not for me—you go ahead. Oh, all right. Just a sip. Hmmm. Ya know, that's not half bad. Kinda blurs the edge of the scotch, without killing it. Huh. We got enough ginger ale?"

We're not sure exactly how a church formerly best known for its dour, Calvinist-Puritan rigor got its name attached to so pleasant a drink. It is, of course, the national church of Scotland. That explains the whisky. But the ginger ale? The history of mixology, murky though it is, tells us that as early as 1895 you would've found this particular product of the chemist's art—even then, it was artificially flavored—associating with brandy and ice. It would've been but a small step to substitute whisky. Small, but necessary: remember phylloxera? (See the **Scotch and Soda**.)

That still doesn't explain the name. No matter. However it got attached, it's an apt one. The history of the Presbyterian Church, both in Scotland and over here, is to a large extent one long struggle between between fundamentalists and moderates, idealists and realists. Whisky, in short, and ginger ale.

Ginger ale to here

Whisky to here

VARIANTS & MIXOLOGY

With half a lime, this becomes a **Mamie Taylor**. Mamie who? Dunno. According to Albert Stevens Crockett's *Old Waldorf Bar Days*, the recipe appeared in the *New York Herald* some time around 1900. But either Crockett didn't know who Ms. Taylor was, or he assumed that everybody did.

Remsen Cooler

A **Scotch and Soda** with a metastasized lemon twist. As we understand it, Remsen was a nineteenth-century brand of Scotch, although we can't tell you much more about it than that. But the darkness that surrounds that 'Remsen' is nothing new: even in the good old days, you'd find some authorities insisting that this one's made with gin. Although, since one of 'em—George J. Kappeler—was writing as far back as 1895, they may be right and we may be wrong. It's been known to happen.

REMSEN COOLER

Put the spiral-cut peel of a whole lemon in a large Collins glass with 2 or 3 ice cubes.

Add 2 oz of Scotch whisky and fill with soda.

Rye and Ginger Ale

Deeply traditional, and with reason: the ginger ale softens the rye's sharp edge without blunting it entirely. Babe Ruth used to drink a quart of these with his breakfast (how else to wash down a sixteen-ounce porterhouse, six fried eggs and a half-acre of homefries?).

RYE AND GINGER ALE

Pour 2 oz rye or Canadian whiskey into a Collins glass, add 2 or 3 ice cubes and top up with ginger ale.

That's one way to cure a hangover. ▶

SCOTCH AND SODA

Pour 2 or 3 oz of blended Scotch into a Collins glass holding 2 or 3 ice cubes and top up with soda.

Note: Whatever you do, for God's sake and ours, don't use a single-malt whisky here—unless you want the thrifty gods who watch over Scotch and its drinkers to smite you hip and thigh and cast your reeking corpse into the outer darkness where all is wailing and gnashing of teeth, and large sebaceous skinheads with names like Angus and Willie and extremely unhealthy diets (think take-away curries and deep-fried frozen pizzas) will use it for their toilet. Forewarned is forearmed.

SCOTCH AND SODA

SCOTCH AND SODA

Pity that America seems to have abandoned its own name for this drink—the **Scotch Highball**—in favor of the bland British appellation for this ever-so-slightly déclassé alternative to the **Brandy and Soda**.

The end of the nineteenth century was a bad time if, like the British upper classes, you were addicted to French brandy. *Phylloxera vastrix*, Prohibition in insect form, had eaten up the roots of just about all the grapevines in Europe, and that included the Charente, the little patch of heaven where they transubstantiate crummy wine into sublime liquor—where, in other words, they make cognac. Rather than drink the suspicious-smelling stuff that was coming over from the Continent, a good many brandy drinkers bit the bullet and fetched an alternative down from the national attic: Scotch whisky, heretofore the bevvy of the wild and kilted (in truth, they already knew it was up there: back in 1848, Queen Victoria took up summer quarters in the Highlands and started a wee craze for things Scottish). Hard times make a monkey eat red peppers, as the saying goes. Once the French situation stabilized, many a gent was too far into the malt to go back.

Victoria, before the bulldog-DNA treatments. ▶

One of the greatest names in mixology, the Singapore Sling is one of those complicated drinks that taste better when you don't have to make them (that doesn't mean, however, that you should go around ordering them in regular bars—lest there be perpetual enmity between thy seed and the seed of bartenders). In its youth, however, the Singapore Sling wasn't quite so fussy. Here, more or less (see below) is how they built them at the Raffles Hotel, Singapore, back before General Yamashita and his army turned the lights out on that particular party.

SINGAPORE SLING

Stir well with 2 or 3 ice cubes:

2 oz London dry gin

½ oz cherry brandy (the sweet kind, as in Cherry Heering)

½ oz Bénédictine

Pour unstrained into Collins glass and fill to taste with cold club soda or seltzer (or a good ginger beer, which really perks this one up). Garnish with the spiral-cut peel of a lime.

Note: There are as many formulae for the Singapore Sling as there are bartenders. The problem is, the original 1915 formula (credited to Ngiam Tong Boon of the Raffles Hotel's Long Bar) is seriously deficient. Calling for equal parts gin, cherry brandy (probably the liqueur type) and Bénédictine and served with the peel of a whole lime and soda, it's sweet to a fault and weird-tasting. Some versions balance the sweetness with citrus juice, others cut one liqueur or the other, still others say the hell with it and dump in whatever fruit juices are under the bar. Some take a more-is-more approach and do all of the above. Result? Libational chaos. Globetrotting tippler Charles Baker, who encountered the drink in 1926, took a more measured approach. He resisted the urge to add citrus juice—with that, it can technically no longer be called a Sling, no matter what some Brits may maintain— and merely adjusted Boon's original proportions to bring out the true nobility lurking behind the stickiness (we've pushed the adjustment a bit further). Although, truth be told, a little lime juice really does help, nomenclature be damned.

11 THINGS WE SIMPLY WILL NOT TRY

1 Red-Headed Slut (Jägermeister, peach schnapps and cranberry juice)

2 Skip and Go Naked (gin, sour mix, grenadine and beer)

3 Vodpacho (vodka and gazpacho)

4 Green Slime (vodka, melon liqueur and lots of barely-stirred egg white)

5 Romulan Ale (no matter what's in it)

6 Yoo-Ha (that's whiskey and Yoo-Hoo)

7 Pousse Café (or anything else consisting of l ers of thick, sticky lique

8 Anything with chu in it

9 Big, Hairy Nut Sack (tequila, rum, egg nog, lime juice, nutmeg and maximum-strength Robitussin—really)

10 Anything invented by a college student

11 White Wine Spritzer

RULE #236

Never order a drink whose name includes a part of the anatomy normally covered by underwear.

COLLINS & COLLINS-LIKE SUBSTANCES

TOM COLLINS

Along with its kissin' cousins, the **Gin Rickey** and the **Gin Fizz**, this classic formula hasn't been getting much exercise of late. Maybe the nasty tang of bottled Collins/sour mix has poisoned virgin taste buds toward the drink, depriving it of the young addicts a cocktail needs to survive. Or maybe it's just a sign of the swath tonic water has cut through summer drinks since its introduction back in the 1930s.

In any case, the Tom Collins nonetheless has on its side tradition—its origins lie in the early-nineteenth century—and simple elegance. Few drinks indeed are as refreshing on a summer afternoon, as Americans used to know—one summer day in 1943, the bar at New York's Hotel Commodore (across from Grand Central Station) served 1,100 of these. And the name? Step one: a certain John Collins, a waiter at Limmer's Old House on London's Hanover Square, gets his name hitched to a drink with lemon, sugar, soda and Holland gin; that must've been around 1810 or 1820. Step two: some bright spark makes same with Old Tom gin and changes the name accordingly. (Since Old Tom gin is a thing of the past, strict-construc-tionists may have theirs this way by adding about ½ oz simple syrup—made 1:1, sugar and water—to a fifth of London Dry gin and cutting back on the sugar in the drink. Pointless, but let us know how they turn out.)

TOM COLLINS

Combine in Collins glass ¾-full of cracked ice:

2 oz London dry gin

1 teaspoon bar sugar

Juice of ½ lemon (George J. Kappeler's 1895 *Modern American Drinks* suggests muddling the lemon half with the sugar before proceeding with the drink—an excellent suggestion)

Stir briefly, top up with club soda or seltzer, garnish with lemon circle and serve with stirring rod.

VARIANTS & MIXOLOGY

These are often made very large—if you've got a glass big enough, double everything. The Collins treatment works well with other liquors: common are the **John Collins**, a.k.a. **Whiskey Collins**, which is self-explanatory, and the **Rum Collins** (light rum) or **Charlie Collins** (Jamaican rum), usually made with a couple dashes of Angostura bitters and lime juice instead of lemon.

GIN RICKEY

Squeeze ½ of a (well-washed) lime into a Collins glass full of ice, add 2 oz London dry gin, throw in the lime half and top up with bubbly water of choice.

That's it. Don't let anybody convince you to put sugar in this. You can use other liquors, adjusting the name accordingly.

Note resemblance to stirring rod. Hmmm. ▶

GIN RICKEY

Back in the Gilded Age, Shoemaker's, on Pennsylvania Avenue in Washington, was–as the 1893 Baedeker's *Handbook to the United States* noted—" a drinking-bar frequented by politicians, journalists, etc." Among the etcetera propping up the bar at the "third Room of the Congress," as it was known, was one Colonel Joe (or Jim; nobody seems to be quite sure) Rickey. The Colonel, described as "a gentleman of grace and charm who wore a black slouch hat above a drooping grey mustache," was neither a politician, nor a journalist, nor, we strongly suspect, a Colonel. He was a lobbyist. As such, he possessed a most useful trait—he was known to be a perfect master of the ancient arts and modern sciences of drinking. If he said a drink was good, it was good. If he said it was lousy, you had the next round elsewhere.

Anyway, one day in the 1890s, a bartender at Shoemaker's handed the Colonel a little something he was working on—which turned out to be perhaps the sole drink known to the mixological arts that can brace one to navigate the Precambrian swamp that is Washington in summer. We don't know the bartender's name. The Colonel went into the lime-importing business. Washington.

MACKINNON

This plucky waif appeared on our doorstep one morning in January, 1938 (at least, that's when Murdock Pemberton included it in his "Potables" column). Oldtimers here at *Esquire* remember how it would make itself useful, sweeping up the day's cigarette butts, delivering the interoffice, nipping out to O'Reilly's around the corner to fetch the junior editors' morning gloom-lifters, that sort of thing. And then there came a day when—

Okay, we'll knock it off. That's right, we don't know a bloody thing about the Mackinnon other than the highly suggestive fact that the family that makes Drambuie, its animating spirit, is named... Mackinnon. Shill job or no, it sure is tasty. The Drambuie's Scotch base contributes just enough of its smokiness to keep things interesting, while its honey-sweetness is beautifully balanced by the citrus juice and drawn out by the soda. And the rum? Not sure, but the drink isn't nearly as good without it. A sleeper.

MACKINNON

Shake well with cracked ice:

2 oz Drambuie

½ oz white rum

½ oz lime juice

½ oz lemon juice

Strain into Collins glass with 2 or 3 ice cubes in it and top off with cold club soda or seltzer.

◄ **We think that's the Mackinnon, there in the window.**

MOJITO

In a smallish Collins glass, muddle juice of ½ lime with ½ teaspoon bar sugar

Add a few mint leaves, mushing them against the side of the glass

Fill glass ⅔ with cracked ice and pour in 2 oz white rum

Pitch in the squeezed-out lime shell and top off with club soda or seltzer (we take ours with a float of dark Jamaica or Demerara rum, which perfumes the drink without weighing it down)

Serve with stirring rod.

The Cuban flag. The white stands for rum, the blue for...ice, the red—aah, to hell with it. ▼

MOJITO

On many a sultry August afternoon, we've given thanks for that attractive force which brings forth the half-breed, the mestizo, the bastard. For the Mojito, you see, is the illegitimate offspring of the tropical **Daiquiri** and the good old Kentucky **Mint Julep**, but taller than either. Well, actually, its bastardy is only metaphorical, since in historical fact the drink has not a lot to do with the Bluegrass State, seeing as all it really is is a stretching-out of the old Cuban **Draque**, or 'Drake' (after Sir Francis), a mix of rum, sugar, lime and mint popular with the working classes since at least the beginning of the nineteenth century. At any rate, this Cuban cooler, which seems to start showing up some time in the 1910s, is a clean, simple drink that lets you get a considerable amount of the creature under your belt with almost no pain or fuss. Hemingway liked 'em, of course—there's a much-touted and doubtless completely unauthentic little jingle about which Havana bar he prefers for Mojitos and which for **Daiquiris**. It's nice to have regular habits and all, but that man would drink anything anywhere. And why not?

VARIANTS & MIXOLOGY

Some—cocktail historian and restaurant critic William Grimes, for one—prefer their Mojitos to be **Draques**, *sin* fizz. You can also make 'em straight up, crushing a sprig of mint thoroughly in the shaker and proceeding as for a **Daiquiri**; if you use lemon juice in this instead of lime, you're drinking a **Cocktail Brugal**, whose formula, once exclusive property of the rum-distilling Brugal family, dates back to the 1880s (you have to use Ron Brugal, of course, which is no hardship; if you don't, call it a **Cool o' the Evening**, as our Lawton Mackall did back in 1945).

THE FIZZ

This class of drinks—basically, liquor, citrus and sweetener shaken together, strained and topped up with carbonated water—dates back to the nineteenth century, when it had something of a reputation as a hangover cure. You really need a soda-siphon to make these right, as they're supposed to be really fizzy. And don't let 'em linger.

CHICAGO FIZZ

The Windy City's contribution to mixology. A genteel drink, obviously from the part of town where Frank Lloyd Wright built houses, not the part where roughnecks butchered pigs and put them in cans.

GIN FIZZ

From the middle of the nineteenth century to the middle of the twentieth, the Gin Fizz was drunk wherever sufferers from that foul affliction, *crapula vulgaris*—to the layman, the common hangover—were found. It goes down easy, anyway. Drink up.

VARIANTS & MIXOLOGY

With champagne, this is known as a **Diamond Fizz**, probably for the way it'll cut through your morning fug. Or, with an egg white, you've got the venerable **Silver Fizz**, a very handsome beverage. Forget the egg white and pretty your Gin Fizz up with a couple sprigs of mint, and that's an **Alabama Fizz**, although Lord knows why.

CHICAGO FIZZ

Shake well with cracked ice:

1 oz Jamaica rum

1 oz port

Generous ½ oz lemon juice

½ teaspoon bar sugar

White of 1 egg (one will do fine for two drinks)

Strain into a chilled small Collins glass and fizz to an inch or so from the top.

GIN FIZZ

Shake well with cracked ice:

2 oz London dry gin

Generous ½ oz lemon juice

1 teaspoon bar sugar

Strain into a chilled small Collins glass and fizz to an inch or so from the top.

GREEN FIZZ

Shake strenuously with cracked ice:

2 oz London dry gin

1 teaspoon green crème de menthe

Generous 1 oz lemon juice

White of 1 egg (one will do fine for two drinks)

1 teaspoon bar sugar

Strain into a chilled small Collins glass and fizz to an inch or so from the top.

◄ **Ebullience in Chicago.**

GREEN FIZZ

In 1949, the unnamed editor(s) of our *Handbook for Hosts* tucked this 1920s Cuban creation away in the "Something for the Girls" section, alongside the **Alexander**, the **Pink Lady**, the **Clover Club** and a few other drinks that might place a man's *cojones* in jeopardy should he be seen ordering them. But upon exhuming this relic and drinking three or four of them (sometimes it takes a little work to get the recipe just right—but you don't want to hear about our problems), we were left with a faint little question mark hanging over our heads. What's so goddamn poofy about the Green Fizz? It's not sweet, there's just a hint of mintiness, and it's pretty potent (and damn refreshing). Sure, it's green, but so are a lot of things. Army uniforms, for one.

Which brings us back to the girls; the ones back then in 1949. They were a pretty tough lot—consider what that perky little 25-year-old already had under her belt. A good ten years of Depression (not the kind you fix with Prozac; the kind where Daddy has no job and everybody eats beans six days a week), followed by four years of scanning the list of dead boys in the morning paper for her classmates' names. Hell, there's a pretty good chance she was in the service herself, bandaging stumps or flying bombers across the Atlantic or what-have-you. So no wonder this so-called girlie drink is about ten times more butch than most of what passes for a manly draught today (why, just last night somebody tried to serve us this *thing* with melon liqueur and raspberry vodka and…oh, forget it).

VARIANTS & MIXOLOGY

For a **Green Swizzle**, mix 3 oz white rum, 1 teaspoon green crème de menthe, ¾ oz lime juice, 1 teaspoon bar sugar and 3 dashes Angostura bitters; strain into Collins glass ¾ full of shaved ice, swizzle it around until the glass frosts and make sure a chair is handy.

HARVARD FIZZ

Tracking recipes for this elegant little brain tonic, one observes that, as the twentieth century progressed, the proportion of brandy to vermouth increased precipitately. It began as three parts weak to two parts strong. By 1946, one finds things running four-to-one the other way. There's a dissertation in there somewhere. We've taken a judicious *via media* in our recipe; adjust according to degree of nostalgia.

RAMOS FIZZ

The Ramos Fizz, alias the **New Orleans Fizz** and the **New Orleans Gin Fizz**, breaks all the rules. It's fussy, dated, takes a long time to make and uses too many ingredients, one quite hard to find. It's not an everyday drink, yet you can't mix it up in big batches for company (nor should you order one in a bar, lest the bartender curse your progeny unto the tenth generation). You've got to make these babies yourself, one or two at a time. So why bother?

If the **Sidecar** is jazz, the Ramos Fizz is ragtime. Sure, it's from New Orleans—cradle of jazz and all that—but it harks back to 1888, two years before Jelly Roll Morton was born and thirteen before Louis Armstrong. Like ragtime, Henry C. Ramos' creation is a matter of poise, of balance, of delicacy. This isn't a drink to throw together from whatever you've got lying around; every part of the formula is crucial. The egg white gives it body, the cream smoothness, the citrus coolth. The sugar tames the citrus, the gin does what gin does, and the seltzer wakes the whole thing up. As for the orange flower water—mystery.

To sip a Ramos Fizz on a hot day is to step into a sepia-toned world peopled with slim, brown-eyed beauties who smell of magnolias and freshly-laundered linen and tall, mustachioed gentlemen who never seem to work and will kill you if you ask them why that is.

HARVARD FIZZ

Stir well with cracked ice:

1½ oz brandy

¾ oz Italian vermouth

Dash of orange bitters

Strain into a chilled small Collins glass and fizz to an inch or so from the top.

RAMOS FIZZ

Combine in shaker with plenty of cracked ice:

2 oz London dry gin

1 oz heavy cream (do not use half-and-half)

White of 1 egg

Juice of ½ lemon

Juice of ½ lime

2 teaspoons bar sugar

2 to 3 drops orange-flower water. Don't bother substituting orange juice or orange liqueur or orange anything else; the orange flower has a fragrance unrelated to that of the fruit. The best brand of orange flower water is Mymouné. (See Last Call on page 188 to order some.)

Shake viciously for at least one minute and preferably two, strain into a chilled Collins glass and fizz to an inch or so from the top.

SLOE GIN FIZZ

Shake well with cracked ice:

2 oz sloe gin

Generous ½ oz lemon juice

1 teaspoon bar sugar

Strain into a chilled small Collins glass and fizz to an inch or so from the top.

Note: Sloe gin? Oh yeah. It's simply sweetened gin that's had sloes (the plumlike fruit of the blackthorn bush) steeped in it. The English brands are by far the best.

SLOE GIN FIZZ

"Its haunting pink color and fruity opulence are topped with a handsome collar of natural foam which, if the sloe gin be of first quality, is gladsome aplenty."

—Lawton Mackall, *Esquire*, August, 1941

TALL & SWEETISH

CUBA LIBRE

In the simplified form of **Rum and Coca-Cola**, this was one of the chief fuels that kept the home fires burning back during the Big One. True, there was hardly anything else to drink—by 1944, just about all American distillers were forking their production over to Uncle Sam, and domestic stocks were low, low, low. Caribbean rum was about the only import plentiful enough to make up for that (things got so bad they were even making gin out of sugarcane, not to mention vodka). The mixer situation wasn't much better. Sugar was rationed, which cut into the market-share of the **Daiquiri** and **Collins** and such, and ginger ale was scarce. Not **Coca-Cola**, though. It's good to be the king.

All the Andrews Sisters bobbysoxer jive aside (don't make us repeat it), the Cuba Libre was already middle-aged. This wasn't its first war, or even its second. The drink was invented, they say, by a Doughboy on occupation duty in Cuba, soon after the Spanish-American war. That was in 1900. "Cuba Libre!" was the rallying cry of the Cuban independence movement, a cause that was quite popular among us *Yanquis*. Sorta the "Free Tibet" of its day, only back then we felt obligated to back up our feel-good sloganeering with battleships and infantry divisions.

Of course, having gotten *libre* from Spain, it took Cuba another sixty-odd years to get *libre* from us. At which point, miffed, we slapped on the embargo, which rendered it illegal to consume an authentic Cuba Libre in either of the countries that produce its two essential components—no Coke in Cuba, no Cuban rum here. But in absolute point of fact, nobody anywhere has been able to drink a Cuba Libre in its full, original glory since about 1901, when the Coca-Cola company started getting nervous about their product's crank factor and began to phase out its not-inconsiderable cocaine content. (Drink archaeologists take note: we really can't endorse any attempts to create a historically-correct Cuba Libre. Wish we could, but there you have it.) But even without that key alkaloid, the drink is a potent little speedball that's way tastier than it has any right to be. Don't leave out the lime, though.

CUBA LIBRE

Squeeze a lime into a Collins glass, add 2 or 3 ice cubes, and pour in 2 oz Cuban or Puerto Rican rum (we like the golden type, and really like a darker, more flavorful riserva such as Bacardi Select)

Drop in one of the spent lime shells and fill with cold **Coca-Cola**

Stir briefly.

This patient responds exceptionally well to Baker's Procedure, something cooked up by Charles H. Baker in his 1939 *Gentleman's Companion*. It requires you to muddle the squeezed-out lime shell in the bottom of the glass before adding the rest of the ingredients, in order to extract a little of the rind's bitter oil. Actually, though, this should be called Kappeler's Procedure, since it was George Kappeler who, in his 1895 *Modern American Drinks*, suggested it be employed to treat the Collins family, then suffering from a slight case of the blahs.

CUBA LIBRE

La Habana, Cuba

FLORODORA

Shake well with cracked ice:

2 oz London dry gin

½ oz lime juice

½ oz raspberry syrup (this can be hard to find; it's a specialty of Eastern Europe, if that's any help)

Pour unstrained into Collins glass and top off with cold ginger ale.

GIN AND TONIC

Combine in Collins glass with 2 or 3 ice cubes:

2 or 3 oz London dry gin

3 to 6 oz tonic water (the kind with quinine)

Garnish with a healthy wedge of lime. This may of course be made with vodka, yielding a serviceable and popular summer cooler but one completely without radiance.

FLORODORA

When "Florodora"—a musical of the most trivial sort—opened at New York's Casino Theatre in 1900, one of the 'sextette' of chorus girls was already secretly married to a millionaire (who happened to peg out opening night, leaving his whole pile to her). Within half a year, each of the other five had landed one of her own. Six girls, six months, six millionaires.

This Waldorf drink's almost as seductive as the Florodora sextette, and you don't have to make a new will before you can enjoy it.

GIN AND TONIC

"The tonic is a sparkling water containing one grain of quinine. Sounds terrible, but wait until you try it! It's the drink of the tropics from the Sailors' Bar at Cartagena to the cool verandah of the Myrtle Bank Hotel at Kingston, Jamaica, and Christophe's Citadel at Milot, Haiti."

—*Handbook for Hosts*, 1949

Little did we know back then that the G and T would go on to single-handedly wipe out all the various **Collinses**, **Fizzes** and **Rickeys** that formerly accounted for the bulk of summer gin consumption.

As much as we revere those old standbys, we can find nothing bad to say about the Gin and Tonic. Whichever Briton it was who, some time around the beginning of the last century, first thought to mix his tropical-issue quinine-water ration with gin, he was a bird of rare sensitivity to the poetry of combining liquids. When the proper proportion the two main ingredients is achieved—a proportion so delicate and subject to subtle variations in their make and quality that we cannot state it exactly—a third something is created that possesses a radiance unsuspected in either of them. Especially in the tonic. (Have you *tried* that stuff straight? Gak!)

MOSCOW MULE

At the beginning of World War II, vodka had a healthy corner of America's exotic-hooch crowd: more than tequila and pisco, less than kirschwasser and barack palinka (Hungarian apricot brandy, to civilians). There were even signs that it was leaching out into the general pool of drinkers, albeit slowly. Too slowly for John G. Martin, the executive for G. F. Heublein (makers of pre-mixed Club Cocktails and Milshire Gin) who had talked them into buying the Smirnoff brand a couple of years back. Vodka needed a signature drink, something simple and fun that would set everyone to drinking it for its own sake. The **Bloody Mary** was a start, but it was still for hangovers only.

Meanwhile, here's Jack Morgan, owner of the Cock 'n' Bull pub, in Hollywood. He's got a problem a lot like Martin's, if on a smaller scale: he's been bottling this nice, spicy ginger beer that nobody wants to drink. One day in 1941, "shortly before Pearl Harbor" (as Morgan later recalled), he and Jack Martin get to talking. The deal is done: Smirnoff, Cock 'n' Bull ginger beer and half a lime (swiped, no doubt, from the **Cuba Libre**), dumped into a special copper mug—another friend with business problems—and stuck with a meaningless but catchy name. The Moscow Mule. A little careful promotion, and wham! Vodka's breakout cocktail. Professional bartenders hated it, but the suckers bit.

At least the Moscow Mule is easy (your dog could make one), smooth and refreshing. Taken by itself, it does no harm, and compared to so much that has followed, it's practically elegant.

Vodka: commie plot? ▼

MOSCOW MULE

Squeeze ½ lime into a Collins glass (or Moscow Mule mug) and drop in the skin

Add 2 or 3 ice cubes, then pour in 2 oz vodka and fill with 4 to 6 oz cold ginger beer (not ginger ale, although what the hell)

Serve with a stirring rod.

VARIANTS & MIXOLOGY

The Moscow Mule is not, by the way, the first silly vodka drink. That distinction belongs to the **Blue Monday**, which you will find under Short Drinks. And by the way—make one of these with a good, dark Bermuda rum, and you've got a **Dark and Stormy**. It beats the bejeezus out of the ol' Mule.

SWINGING CHAD

Stir well with cracked ice:

2 oz golden Puerto Rican (or, of course, Cuban) rum

2 oz unsweetened pineapple juice

2 dashes Angostura bitters

1 dash Pernod

Pour unstrained into Collins glass and top off with ginger ale. Supply a straw and garnish with a paper umbrella into which you have cut a few little rectangular holes (use an x-acto knife—and if you're going to have more than one, best to prep all the umbrellas beforehand).

SWINGING CHAD

One morning in the midst of the late spasm of electoral dysfunction we received a communication from Hardwicke, a young man employed in our research department. It seems that, while spooling through the microfilmed morgue of the West Palm Beach *Clarion-Shopper*, he came across a curious item from way back in 1960—when those punch-card machines that got our national seams so crooked were as new-fangled as the latest version of Windows, and just about as efficient.

The article Hardwicke came up with deals with 'chads' and those who, for want of a better word, sex them. A chad, you'll surely recall, is that little rectangle of paper that falls out when you punch a punch-card. Or fails to fall out, disconcertingly often. In which case you have to classify it—is it a hanging chad (one corner attached)? A swinging chad (two corners), a tri-chad (three)? Or is it merely a pregnant chad, a little bulgy in the middle but all four corners hanging on. Thirsty work, deciding all that.

The chad-sexers in 1960 thought so, anyway, and—according to the *Clarion-Shopper*—one of them decided to do something about it. It is to Mrs. Ivy Gelbfisch, a 53-year-old Democratic precinct captain from Palm Beach Lakes (though originally from Bayonne), that we owe this little lubricant for the wheels of democracy. It has since become the traditional tipple of the Florida vote-counter. Ivy, wherever you are, a grateful nation salutes you. (And if you're still with us, we know your chads were punched clean.)

VARIANTS & MIXOLOGY

Variations: for the **Tri-chad**, replace the ginger ale with club soda and add ½ oz triple-sec (or Cointreau); for the **Hanging Chad**, make a Swinging Chad and float ½ oz 151-proof Demerara rum on top. For the Pregnant Chad— we don't do sex drinks here at *Esquire*.

◀ **Was it the chad?**

CONSPICUOUS CONSUMPTION, OR CHAMPAGNE

AIR MAIL (A.K.A. RUM FLYER)

AIR MAIL (A.K.A. RUM FLYER)

Mix thoroughly in shaker:

2 oz golden Puerto Rican rum

Juice of ½ lime

1 teaspoon honey

Add cracked ice, shake well and pour unstrained into Collins glass

Fill with iced brut champagne.

AIR MAIL

We owe this obscure but potent little almagoozlum—a cross between the **FRENCH 75** and the **HONEY BEE**—to the nice folks at Bacardi, in whose 1930s-era pamphlet, "Bacardi and its Many Uses," it appears as if by spontaneous generation. Back then, of course, airmail was the last word in getting something from point A to point B. And in fact, this one'll do just that to you, but quick. So quick that, if we were inclined to take such liberties, we'd rename it the "E-mail."

BLACK VELVET

Half-fill a Collins glass with stout and top up slowly with iced brut champagne

Stir gently with glass or plastic rod.

BLACK VELVET

London: Brookes's Club, Sunday, December 15, 1861.

… morning, damn its eyes … "Barman!" *… what's the poxy little blighter's name again? … no matter …* "Here, barman! A pint of 'the boy!'" *… champagne … only thing for a head like this …* "Hi! Quick about it, now." *… mustn't drink punch … worst thing … o thank god … almost here … steady on, man, don't spill it … but why the 'that's-simply-not-done-sir' air? … black velvet band on his arm … old Brinsley, over there—he's got the same …* "Who's dead, then?" …

"Have you not heard, sir? It is the Prince, the Queen's Consort—last night, of a fever, they say."

… o Christ no …can't be seen drinking bloody champagne … still, only thing … head like this … never cared much for the fellow anyway … Prince Albert … bit of a prig … poor bloody queen … mad for him…

"I suppose champagne really won't do, will it?"

"No, sir."

"Can't you put a bit of that black velvet around the bloody glass or something?"

"If I might be permitted to suggest, sir, a portion of black Irish stout added to the wine will effectively darken its colour."

… hulloa, what was that? …

"It is as Shakespeare says, sir: 'coal-black is better than another hue, in that it scorns to bear another hue.'"

… clever little bugger …

"Shall I proceed, sir?"

"Anything, man, can't you see I'm bl—dashed desperate."

… look at that, black as a Newcastle collier … easy now, drink it down … damned tasty, actually … bollocks, here's Flashman … £400 of mine in his pocket, the blackguard … mustn't drink punch at the tables, mustn't, mustn't, mustn't …

"Hulloa, Calverton. Where's your black velvet?"

… insolent … "I'm drinking it."

ERNEST HEMINGWAY'S DEATH IN THE AFTERNOON

There's a bit near the beginning of Vergil's *Georgics* (in which Imperial Rome's greatest poet versifies, at length, on the art of farming; weird, but no weirder than, say, David Foster Wallace) where he imagines a peasant, busting sod on an old battlefield, turning up the bones of some of the slaughtered—and they're huge. That's how we feel contemplating Hemingway's original instructions for this wicked potion (he claims to have cooked it up with some Brits after a spot of nautical unpleasantness): "Pour 1 jigger of absinthe into a champagne glass. Add iced champagne until it attains the proper opalescent milkiness. Drink 3 to 5 of these slowly." The liver that man must've had! Giants did indeed walk among us.

Unfortunately, absinthe's still illegal here. But if you find yourself in Europe and your better half has just left you, perhaps citing your persistent sniggering at her (or his, *bien sûr*) ostentatious mastery of the local parley-voo, you might want to embark on a course of these. You can get real absinthe there—and, seeing as how it has a tendency to taste like bug-killer, the champagne can only help it. Just make sure you leave your documents and most of your money in the hotel safe before you commence treatment.

Himself. ▶

DEATH IN THE AFTERNOON

Pour into champagne flute:

1½ oz absinthe (the Spanish stuff, for authenticity)

Add iced brut champagne until it clouds up—at least 4 oz.

NEAR-DEATH VARIANTS & MIXOLOGY

If you lack the kind of decadent friends who engage in pretentious pursuits like smuggling absinthe, there are a couple of legal alternatives for getting your mitts on the stuff (see the **Absinthe Frappé**). For what our own Brendan Vaughan has christened the **Near-Death Experience**, use Absente, the new, legal, absinthe substitute that's been promoted of late; it's 110 proof (the real stuff is always real strong, whatever its other attributes). If you prefer to keep the Man in Black safely at arm's length, try using a mere ounce of Pernod or other 80-proof pastis. Let's call that the **Paper Cut**.

FRENCH 75

Shake well with cracked ice:

2 oz London dry gin

1 teaspoon bar sugar

¾ oz lemon juice

Strain into Collins glass half-full of cracked ice, and top off with brut champagne—about 5 oz.

MIMOSA

Fill champagne flute ⅔ full (or ⅓, for Anglophiles) of fresh-squeezed orange juice and top up with Brut champagne.

Dash in a little Grand Marnier, if you like.

VARIANTS & MIXOLOGY

For a true **Buck's Fizz**, add a touch of grenadine; for a true Mimosa, it's a touch of Grand Marnier (not enough, we're afraid, to compensate for the champagne deficit). In either case, a dash of orange bitters, if you have them, will add a little complexity to this exceedingly simple drink. Sometimes, though, you want—need—simplicity.

FRENCH 75

The 75-millimeter M1897 was the mainstay of the French field artillery in World War I, a light, potent little gun with a vicious rate of fire. Hence the drink. Of all the many champagne-and-liquor combinations known to contemporary mixology, this one has the most élan. Two of these and you'd fight to defend Madonna's honor. The drink was a favorite of the Lost Generation—hell, there's enough alcohol in it to give even Hemingway a buzz.

Most modern recipes lowball the gin in here; one online compendium cuts it down to 1/4 oz. For shame. Nor should one adulterate this old soldier with Cointreau or the like. No shame, however, in leaving out the gin entirely—as long as you replace it with brandy or cognac (yielding a **King's Peg**, although these generally omit the lemon and sugar).

MIMOSA

Two drinks, both alike in dignity, both served at brunch. Each dates to the 1920s, each mixes champagne with orange juice—they're the same drink, more or less. In America, we call it a Mimosa; in England, it's a **Buck's Fizz**. Who's right? As Americans, let's just say there is no right or wrong in this situation; it's simply a case of they say 'tomahto' and we say 'potayto.' In other words, they've got us, the swine. Far as we can tell, the **Buck's Fizz** was first poured in 1921 at London's Buck's Club, by one Pat McGarry, barman (at any rate, it turns up in the 1930 *Savoy Cocktail Book*). The Mimosa's roots are said to reach to Paris's Ritz Hotel, a couple of years later in that decade.

But that's not the worst of it. Not only did we back the slow horse, we backed the weak one. It's a question of proportions: the French version, with a typical continental aversion for alcohol, prescribes two parts orange juice to one of champagne. The Brits, not surprisingly, reverse that proportion.

But whatever you call it, whether you favor club or shrub, this is the gentlest of brunch drinks: as theoretical mixologist David Embury put it in his 1958 *Fine Art of Mixing Drinks*, "It is not half bad and the ladies usually like it."

PINT-SIZED PUNCHES

CAPE CODDER

This one seems to date to sometime in the 1960s, although it does bear more than a passing resemblance to the rum-and-cranberry **Cape Cod Collins** that Crosby Gaige included in his 1944 *Standard Cocktail Guide*. By 1972, anyway, Trader Vic was able to include two versions of the vodka Cape Codder in his *Bartender's Guide, Revised*. What's more, it bears an uncanny resemblance to the **Rangoon Ruby**, found in his 1968 *Pacific Island Cookbook*—and in the 1967 *Booze*, a mod little drinks collection put out by a couple of Washington society hostesses. Did they pirate it from the Trader? No idea.

When we first encountered the Cape Codder, in the early 1980s, it was generally found in the company of the kind of out-of-college ash-blonde who favors twin sets and sensible shoes and works in publishing.

VARIANTS & MIXOLOGY

In the fullness of time, the preppy Cape Codder begat the even-preppier **Madras** (named, no doubt, after the favorite plaid of the Ivy-League undergraduate, not the Subcontintental city), which is prepared thus: mix 2 oz vodka and 2 oz O.J. in a Collins glass, slip in a couple of ice cubes and float 2 oz of cranberry juice; serve with stirrer and, if you wish, wedge of lime (people like something to play with). In the fuller fullness of time, the Madras begat the **Cosmopolitan**, which brings us pretty much up to date. Oh yeah, that **Rangoon Ruby**? Cape Codder with juice of ½ lime.

CAPE CODDER

Pour 2 oz vodka (or white rum) into a Collins glass, add 2 or 3 oz cranberry juice cocktail, the juice of half a lime (some leave this out) and a couple of ice cubes

Top off with club soda or seltzer (some leave this out, too, doubling the cranberry; we don't)

Garnish, if you wish, with a slice of lime and/or a sprig of mint.

FLORIDA PUNCH

Shake well with cracked ice:

1½ oz dark Jamaica rum

¾ oz brandy

1½ oz grapefruit juice

1½ oz orange juice

Strain into Collins glass filled with cracked ice

Garnish with plastic flamingo or palm tree. What the hell.

FLORIDA PUNCH

Florida Punch is to **Mississippi Punch** as Florida is to Mississippi: higher I.Q., lower R.Q. (Redneck Quotient). The recipe dates to at least—well, we're not sure. But sometimes we like a high R.Q., and sometimes, alas, we don't.

MAI TAI

Mixology isn't organic chemistry—wait a sec. Mixology is organic chemistry. Then that puts Victor J. Bergeron—Trader Vic, to his public—in the scientific pantheon somewhere between Lavoisier (Father of Modern Chemistry) and John Styth Pemberton, the cracker who came up with **Coca-Cola.** On the basis of the Mai Tai, closer to the French guy.

In 1944, as the Russians were pulverizing Hitler's Army Group Center and the Anglo-Saxons were forcing their way through the Normandy hedgerows and over the bloody coral ridges of Saipan, Bergeron surveyed the state of the world from behind the bar of Hinky Dink's, his restaurant in Oakland, California. "I felt a new drink was needed," he later wrote. Yes.

He began with a fine, 17-year-old Jamaican rum. But let's let him tell it. "I took a fresh lime, added some orange curaçao from Holland, a dash of Rock Candy Syrup, and a dollop of French orgeat, for its subtle almond flavor. A generous amount of shaved ice and vigorous shaking by hand produced the marriage I was after. Half the lime shell went in for color.... I stuck in a branch of fresh mint and gave two of them to Ham and Carrie Guild, friends from Tahiti.... Carrie took one sip and said, '*Mai tai—roa aé!*' In Tahitian this means 'Out of this world—the best!'"

Oh how the Mai Tai has suffered, not the least at Bergeron's own hands. Success brought shortages and substitutions (the fine old rum was the first to go, followed by the imported orgeat), more success brought shortcuts and mass production and inept imitation. Eventually, this divine compound was reduced to a bottled mix or a what-the-hey catchall for stray fruit juices and grades of rum a pirate would have trouble choking down. But when the experiment is performed correctly, just for a minute you forget that things like World Wars exist or are even possible. Out of this world indeed.

MAI TAI

Stir well with cracked ice:

2 oz aged Jamaican rum (Appleton's reserve) or 1 oz Myers's and 1 oz aged Martinique rum

½ oz orange curaçao

½ oz orgeat syrup (that almond stuff baristas have been known to inflict on coffee; for all we know, you can pick some up at your local Starbucks)

⅛ oz "rock candy syrup" (this is no more than sugar syrup—look it up in your *Joy of Cooking*—made with a couple drops of vanilla; don't worry, it's not essential)

Juice of 1 lime

Shake well and pour unstrained (if making two or more, easier to strain it into the glasses and then pour in the ice left in the shaker) into a large Collins glass (or, of course, Tiki mug)

Garnish with half lime shell and sprig of mint.

▲ **Unsanitary doings at Trader Vic's, ca. 1944.**

MILK PUNCH

Stir well with cracked ice (if you shake it, it'll foam):

2 oz dark Jamaican rum (or any full-bodied, naval-type rum)

1 teaspoon bar sugar

6 to 8 oz whole milk

Strain into large goblet or Collins glass. Sprinkle with nutmeg, if you like nutmeg.

You don't have to make this with rum, of course: any of the dark liquors (whiskey, brandy) will work just fine (just don't try it with tequila—or do; what's it to us?). For **Bull's Milk**, use 1½ oz of brandy flavored with ½ oz dark rum and try not to think about stock breeding. And if you're in the realm of Old Man Winter, "sullen and sad, with all his rising train—vapours, clouds and storms" (quoth the poet), few mixtures are as warming as **Hot Milk Punch**: in a mug (any kind, as long as it doesn't have a picture of Garfield or Dilbert on it—show some class), mix 1 oz dark Jamaican rum, 1 oz brandy and a teaspoon bar sugar; fill with hot milk and sprinkle a few grains of nutmeg on top.

MILK PUNCH

> ❝ **As served on rolling days at sea and a rainy day in Colon, Panama.** ❞

Somebody here at *Esquire* hung that tag on the Milk Punch in our 1949 *Handbook for Hosts*. We've got no earthly idea what he was on about. But the guys who used to drink for us, they were always, well, um… Okay, they were writers. The kind who churned out things like plays, short stories, novels, memoirs.

You tell these guys to do something simple and you get, well, writing. Frank Shay, Murdock Pemberton, Lawton Mackall, George Frazier (not the pugilist), Scott Hart, Frederic Birmingham: men who wouldn't bat an eyelash at deploying a word like "interjubilation" or suggesting that you shake a drink "as though 7 demons were goading you to it" (and not the personal kind, we might add). Which is to say—Colon, Panama? We'd be drinking something involving the commingling of rum, lime juice and ice, rain or no. But if those rileys felt like Milk Punch, we're sure they knew what they were doing.

Milk Punch is one of the more ancient medications in the pharmacopoeia. They drank it in Colonial times, they drank it in Boston, they drank it on the Mississippi riverboats, they drank it just about everywhere, right on through the Second World War. After that, America seems to have lost the taste. We can still recall our own naïve revulsion upon witnessing Barnaby Jones order a Scotch and Milk (an elemental milk punch also favored by Walt 'Pogo' Kelly and Dizzy 'Dizzy' Gillespie). We were wrong—although we still prefer it with rum or brandy or both (which last, one of the most voluptuous and comforting of all drinks, has been known to travel under the distasteful moniker of **Bull's Milk**). And no, you can't use skim milk, or soy milk. Grow up.

MISSISSIPPI PUNCH

> " *Whoooo-eeeeee! I see drunk people.* "

Eyeball what goes into this particular intoxicant—a hefty four ounces of cognac, bourbon and rum—and it's clear where its origins lie: somewhere on Ole Miss' fraternity row, probably in the go-go 1980s (cognac ain't cheap). The mother of all frat drinks.

Well, not quite—at least 120 years' worth of not quite. The recipe for Mississippi Punch actually dates back to the *Bon Vivant's Companion* by 'Professor' Jerry Thomas, "the greatest bartender in American history," as pulp journalist Herbert Asbury called him. That first came out in 1862. But the drink's probably even older than that. Consider the origins of its ingredients: French cognac, American bourbon, Jamaican—and therefore British—rum, Mediterranean— and therefore Spanish—lemons and sugar. It's Mississippi history in a glass, de Soto, Louis XIV, Bull Connor and all. The only folks showing the good sense to stay out of this one are the Chickasaws.

So what we're driving at here is that the overcharge of alcohol just means Mississippi Punch is old enough to reflect the time this country was *really* rowdy. But the funny thing is, this is a truly delicious drink. Not one to pour down your gullet in squadrons, but a supremely smooth slow-sipper that, some-how, doesn't *taste* like it's all firewater.

MISSISSIPPI PUNCH

Shake well with cracked ice:

2 oz cognac or other French brandy

1 oz bourbon

1 oz dark Jamaica rum

½ oz lemon juice

2 teaspoons bar sugar

Strain into Collins glass ⅔-full of cracked ice, garnish with fruit—a slice of orange and a few raspberries, if they're in season, should do it—and attack with straws. (There's a little problem with Thomas's recipe, honesty compels us to admit: it calls for a wineglass of cognac and half-wineglasses of bourbon and rum; now, he doesn't say how much a wineglass is, but it's normally 4 oz. We have, however, seen it quantified as 2 oz; on the advice of our legal department, we went with that. But if the professor really did mean for this baby to hold 8 oz of liquor, well, God Bless America.)

OLD DELAWARE FISHING PUNCH

Shake well with cracked ice:

2 oz light-bodied Barbados rum

1 oz brandy

1 teaspoon lemon juice

1 teaspoon lime juice

1 teaspoon bar sugar

Strain into Collins glass ⅔-full of cracked ice and top off with not-too-much club soda. Garnish with lemon wheel and sip—*slowly.*

OLD DELAWARE FISHING PUNCH

Old, pleasant and completely unassuming—the perfect companion for an afternoon out on the lake (unless you're the kind of person who has a full bar onboard, you might want to bottle a bunch of these in advance, using plain water instead of fizz). Watch your balance, though: this soft-spoken nineteenth-century gent can cut up rough if dissed.

PALE DEACON

Shake well with cracked ice:

3 oz London dry gin

4½ oz fresh-squeezed grapefruit juice (if you're building a bunch of these, an electric juicer is a decided asset; and if you want to use the stuff in the carton—after the first round, folks'll have other things to worry about)

½ teaspoon bar sugar

Pour unstrained into chilled Collins glass.

PALE DEACON

Jack F. Zimmerman, of Akron, Ohio, sent this in to our December, 1936 "Potables" column. We sorta lost track of him after that. Too bad, if only because we're kinda curious as to the results of long-term consumption of this potent little wonder.

Piña Colada

Some drinks make themselves indispensable. What would one-night stands with junior account reps down here—Miami, San Juan, Atlanta; wherever here may be—for the convention be without the P.C.? An empty formality, devoid of joy and, more important, stripped of that pleasant haze of forgetfulness in which fond memories so easily take root.

This Puerto Rican invention of the 1950s or 1960s (there are competing claims) is one of those drinks you really should leave to the bartenders: it's hard for them to screw up, and they've got the right kind of blender and all the garnishes right there in front of them. But if you must …

Suggested presentation... ▶

PIÑA COLADA

Combine in blender:

> 2 oz golden Puerto Rican rum
>
> 3 oz unsweetened pineapple juice (or 3 oz crushed—or whole—pineapple)
>
> 1 oz coconut cream (not coconut juice or milk; you want the sweetened stuff with the chemicals—Coco Lopez is traditional)

Blend on high with 5 or 6 ice cubes (add them 1 or 2 at a time, through the hole in the lid) and pour into tall glass, preferably one of those silly ones with the short stem. You know, like the one you stole from that dumb bar during your last convention?

Garnish with—hell, whatever you've got. Fruit. For extra eye-appeal, float ½ oz cherry liqueur on top, pouring it in over the back of a spoon. Go for it.

PLANTER'S PUNCH

Stir well with cracked ice:

3 oz Jamaica rum

Scant juice of 1 lime

½ oz lemon juice

½ oz grenadine

¼ teaspoon bar sugar

Strain into Collins glass ⅔-full of cracked ice; stick a straw in it and garnish with whatever you want.

PLANTER'S PUNCH

Stripping off the white-linen suit and Panama hat, laying aside the panatella and the silver-headed malacca cane, the Planter's Punch is just another rum-sugar-citrus drink (see the **Daiquiri**, the **Mojito** and the **Caipirinha**). In 1930, the English traveler Alec Waugh described the "ritual of mixing a Creole punch" thus: "quarter of a finger's height of sugar, two fingers high of rum, the paring of a lime, the rattling of ice." That's about it, for the basic version. Not fascinating, but as long as you use a decent dark rum—Jamaica, Barbados, Martinique—distinctly palatable.

But that's not the whole story. There are variations: with orange juice, with grenadine, with curaçao, with Angostura bitters, with just about anything vaguely Caribbean—even cayenne pepper. Garnishes range from none to sensible to amusing to ridiculous. In fact, the plain old Planter's Punch has become an umbrella drink.

There's no shame in that. Not much, anyway. Man cannot live by the stemmed glass alone: sometimes there must be a Tiki mug. So put on your Hawaiian Punch hat, turn Martin Denny up on the hi-fi and give out with the "How low can you go?" Here's Trader Vic's recipe from 1947; it's a killer. And dig the crazy color.

...(just kidding).

STONE FENCE

To be distinguished from a **Stone Wall**, which is an obsolete American moniker for the **Brandy and Soda**, this is a potent draught of some antiquity. Washington Irving mentions it, or *something* called a Stone Fence—a name which hints at the effect produced by getting outside too many of these, which is not unlike that produced by running downhill into one.

ZAMBOANGA MONKEY TAIL

Finding ourselves one day in Oxnard, California, with a few minutes to kill, we wandered into the Salvation Army store. There, among the yellow self-help books and coverless romance novels, we spied a battered copy of Trader Vic's 1946 *Book of Food and Drink*. This fell out, written in a clear hand on the bottle-stained half of an airmail envelope.

▼ **Don't mess with the tail. Really.**

STONE FENCE

Pour into pint glass:

2 oz Scotch whisky (in Irving's day, applejack, brandy, rum or rye, in order of popularity)

Add 1 or 2 ice cubes and fill with hard cider.

ZAMBOANGA MONKEY TAIL

2 oz dark Jamaican rum

½ oz kirschwasser (dry cherry brandy)

1 oz lime juice

1 oz pineapple juice

Dash of orange bitters

½ teaspoon simple syrup and ½ teaspoon grenadine (1 teaspoon of straight grenadine will work just as well)

Shake with crushed ice, strain into Collins glass (or Tiki mug) ⅔-full of shaved ice and garnish with lime shell and mint.

Sure, it's a knockoff of the **Mai Tai**. But it's not half bad. Oxnard, a thirsty nation salutes you.

ZOMBIE

1 oz white rum

1½ oz golden Puerto Rican rum

1 oz dark Jamaican rum

½ oz 151–proof rum (preferably Demerara, if you can find it)

Juice of one lime

½ oz pineapple juice

1 teaspoon papaya juice (this is what mixologist David Embury calls the "mystery ingredient:" it can be passion-fruit nectar, coconut milk, apricot or cherry brandy, just about anything this side of Romilar—although…. It doesn't matter, since you can't taste it anyway)

1 teaspoon bar sugar

Stir together all these ingredients except the 151

Pour into 14-oz. glass which has been filled ¾-full of cracked ice

Float the 151-proofer as a lid—pour it into a spoon and gently lower it under the surface of the drink (if the spirit moves you to light this, it will burn)

Garnish with mint (either straight or dipped in lime juice and then bar sugar) and/or fruit (particularly fetching: take a toothpick and impale a lemon slice or pineapple cube between two maraschino cherries, lay this over the top of the drink)

Supply a straw and, after two, a hammock (after three: a stretcher).

ZOMBIE

The Zombie is the mother of all freak drinks. Although it may seem like a product of the Pu-Pu platter 1950s, it actually hearkens back to the late 1930s, when Hollywood restaurateur Don the Beachcomber supposedly cooked it up as liquid CPR for some poor SOB experiencing death by hangover—thereby delivering him into the clutches of Baron Samedi (you know, the bald guy in *Live and Let Die*). In any case, it caught on, especially at the Hurricane Bar at the 1939 New York World's Fair (perhaps that explains the Trylon and Perisphere). By the time Tiki culture hit its stride, the Zombie, with all its evil, only-two-to-a-customer charms, was ubiquitous. Unfortunately, that didn't mean that it was particularly good. In fact, it's not. But no matter—sometimes the need will strike anyway. We can respect that.

Our crack laboratory staff here at *Esquire*, after five rounds of destructive testing—and believe you me, they were pretty thoroughly destroyed, even Pete, who somehow managed to…aahhh, never mind—have been brought to the verdict (well, carried, actually) that the Zombie is not for home consumption. If you absolutely, positively must crawl into the Z-Hole, let a member of the brotherhood of the black vest perform the necessary rites. At least that way you won't have all those empty rum bottles to hide. But if you like Zombies, you're really not the type to heed sensible advice, are you? So here's a recipe (nobody has *the* recipe).

THE MISCELLANEOUS FILE (INCLUDING BEER)

ABSINTHE FRAPPÉ

"The Absinthe Drinker: him, too, I knew in New York. He was good-looking in a pallid sort of way, a slender, tallish young man, a dilettante in letters…. In the Cafe Martin, Twenty-sixth Street and Fifth Avenue, at four o'clock, we spent a hundred afternoons, listening to the music, watching the people, desultorily talking, and looking upon the absinthe in its cold, sinister, death-colored seduction.

The Drinker drank eight absinthe frappés in the hour [holy cow!—ed.], while I ambled through one. 'To think', said I in half-sad protest, 'that it's slowly killing you, that you've been slowly dying for two years and are slowly dying now!' And said he quickly, 'But, my child, what a sweet, sweet death to die! We are all dying, you know, from one cause or another—we are all, in this orchid-decked room, slowly moving toward our graves. So how much better to go with this exquisite poison in our veins, with the taste of it on our lips, and the flavor of it in our hearts!'"

On July 25, 1912, two years after Mary MacLane (see the **Dubonnet Cocktail**) wrote those words, the Department of Agriculture banned absinthe. Whether this was due to this spring-green, wormwood-infused stomach tonic's harmful physical effects (it clocked in at 120 proof), its reputation as a mild hallucinogen or its capacity to inspire pretentious gothic twaddle, we don't know.

Up until recently, that's as far as absinthe went—a hot-rails-to-hell-and-I-don't-care-who-knows-it historical curiosity. Just about the only place it was legal was

▲ **Absinthe-sipping loony Arthur Rimbaud in full goth mode.**

ABSINTHE FRAPPÉ

Pour into blender:

1 oz absinthe

½ tablespoon bar sugar (the quantity will need to be adjusted according to the brand of absinthe, as they vary greatly in sweetness)

1 oz water

Blend for a moment to dissolve the sugar and then, with the blender running, add 3 or 4 ice cubes through the hole in the top of the blender, pausing between them to let them get crushed

Blend until smooth and pour into whatever odd or archaic glassware you've got.

Spain, and they weren't exporting any. Then came the European Economic Community, which has this odd idea that you shouldn't be able to ban things one place and not another. So now there are dozens of brands on the market, most understrength compared to the original stuff and all deficient in thujone—the THC of absinthe (more EEC regs). You still can't buy it here, though. (There are plenty of legal substitutes, old—Pernod, which used to be the biggest producer of the good stuff; New Orleans' cleverly-named Herbsaint—and new—Absente, La Muse Verte. They're almost all sweeter than real absinthe, and none has that unmistakable wormwood taste.)

True absinthe is bitter, verging on unpleasant. Should you find yourself loitering in the vicinity of a bottle (the Spanish is still the best), there are basically two ways you can go to deal with this. There's the ritual way: you pour an ounce or so of absinthe into your short-stemmed, heavy-bottomed absinthe glass, you lay your spade-shaped, perforated absinthe spoon over its mouth, place one of those double-sized French sugar cubes on it and dribble cold water through the sugar until the glass is full and the sugar crumbly, admiring the way the absinthe gets all cloudy as you pour. Then you dump the sugar into the glass and hack at it with the spoon until it's dissolved. This is fine, if you like arts and crafts. Then there's the good way. The frappé.

ABSINTHE HOME BREW

If you don't go in for globetrotting, you can make your own absinthe without too much fuss. Crush 1½ oz anise seed with mortar and pestle or food processor. Add 1 oz dried wormwood (*artemisia absinthium*; you can get it from your local herbalist) and ⅛ oz hyssop (back to the herbalist). Stir this into 1 quart grain alcohol. (Option: add 10 sprigs fresh mint.) Seal it tight and let it stand two to three weeks, being sure to shake it up at least once a day. Pour the liquid through a coffee filter into a 2-quart container. Add 24 oz distilled water to the macerated herbs, stir well, and filter it into the alcohol. Let this settle, filter it again, leaving out the dregs, add at least 1 cup of simple syrup (made by bringing 1 cup sugar and ½ cup water to a boil, stirring for a minute, and letting it cool) and bottle it up.

This recipe is far from perfect—without a home still, which we don't recommend (word to the wise: revenooers), you can't really turn out a suave product. But it's plenty strong, and it'll do what absinthe is supposed to do—induce a mild, echo-y pot-like high. It's very bitter, though. Many of your friends will suspect you're trying to pizen 'em. Which reminds us: as master mixologist George J. Kappeler warned in 1895, "the free use of absinthe is injurious; never serve it in any kind of drink unless it is called for by the customer."

BOILERMAKER

Nothing mystifying about this—**a shot of whiskey with a beer chaser**—beyond the name and the ability some folks we know have to absorb these without seeming effect.

This is one drink no bartender in Christendom can screw up. If it's Scotch ye be chasin', that used to be called an **L.G.** ("Note: favourite drink up in Scotland with the Labour M.P.'s"—Harry MacElhone, *Harry's ABC of Mixing Cocktails*, ca. 1925). On the other hand, a **K.G.**, named after the artist Kenneth Goldsmith, is merely an Old-Fashioned glass half-full of the best cognac or armagnac you can procure.

CINCINNATI COCKTAIL

To mix a Cincinnati Cocktail, **pour a pint glass half-full of beer and top it off with soda water.** Why you would want to do this, we'll get to in a minute. First, why Cincinnati?

Far as we can tell, the name's a joke—on the order of, as one of our correspondents points out, 'Staten Island whitefish', which is a used condom floating in the water. Back before World War I, when sauerkraut suddenly turned into 'liberty cabbage', Cincinnati was known for its immense and very out German population (they even taught the public schools *auf Deutsch*). And Germans drink beer. So, if you make a cocktail with beer... We said it was a joke; we didn't say it was funny. It is, however, really quite refreshing.

And that's why you drink it. Use a good, full-flavored microbrew, and it'll be better than any lite beer ever attempted, and just as thirst-quenching. Some of the early authorities (the drink goes back to the 1880s) suggest you cut your beer with lemon soda or ginger ale. That, we don't recommend (although English ale and ginger beer, when mixed, produce the classic, and tasty, **Shandy Gaff**).

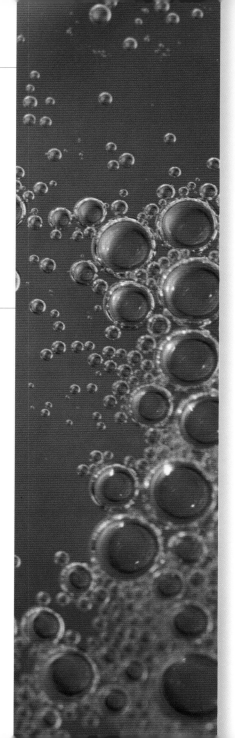

DOG'S NOSE

Drop or pour a shot glass of London dry gin into a pint of porter, pale ale or bitter.

PASTIS

Pour 2 oz of Pernod, Ricard, Pastis 51 or the like into a small Collins glass

Serve with a small pitcher or flask of chilled mineral water (the flat kind) on the side, for dilution

Splash in a bit and watch things cloud up. Poetic, *hein*?

SANGRITA

Mix:

8 oz fresh-squeezed orange juice

1 oz lime juice

1 teaspoon grenadine

Hot sauce to taste (something fiery and Mexican, if possible, although Tabasco works fine; in either case, the final product should produce a pronounced burn)

Chill and serve in shot glasses, with the best tequila you can afford.

DOG'S NOSE

We're throwing in this old English curiosity 'cause we like the name. You try it. Cold and wet, anyway.

Question: hot or cold? Here's Dickens, from *The Pickwick Papers*: "warm porter, moist sugar, gin, and nutmeg." But his contemporary, Elizabeth Gaskell, describes it in *Sylvia's Lovers* as a "mug of beer, into which a noggin of gin had been put (called in Yorkshire 'dog's-nose'),'" and treats it as a refreshing draught. If pressed, we suppose, we'd go with the girls on this one. But really now, who cares?

PASTIS

The characteristic drink of the kind of Frenchman who goes about in a flat blue cap—but not to be shunned for that.

SANGRITA

Mexico isn't like other countries. And it certainly isn't like its big, goofy neighbor to the north. For one thing, the strange, cool, frightening world of the Aztecs and the Maya is a lot closer to the surface than Salma Hayek and the Taco Bell dog lead us to believe. Case in point, Sangrita. When you say "a shot and a chaser" to a gringo, that chaser's gonna pop up in his—or her—head as a beer. Even if you specify that the shot's gonna be tequila. And if you said the chaser wasn't beer and set your bibulous pals guessing, it'd be a long, long time before they came up with something like this. This "little blood"—the meaning of sangrita—is a left-field combo of orange juice, lime juice, grenadine—and hot sauce. Weird. Taste it, though, and it makes perfect sense. *Viva Montezuma!*

AND FINALLY, THE JULEP

MINT JULEP

In the dark backward of time, the Proper Construction of the Julep, like the Beauty of My State's Women and the Timing of Pickett's Charge, was one of those topics that an American male with social aspirations was expected to regard as a matter of honor—at least, if said specimen was a son, nephew, cousin or acquaintance of the South. Just about every state in Dixie had its own sacrosanct way of handling the mint, the sugar, the ice, the booze. Duels were fought. Names were called.

Brushing aside all the tedious to-and-fro about brandy, rum and rye (before the War between the States, a true Southern gentleman would be hanged before he'd let whiskey pass his lips, and even after, when standards had slipped, no Marylander would build his Julep with anything but rye), it's the mint that caused most of the trouble. The question: whether to muddle the mint or slide it into the glass altogether unmolested.

At the beginning of the twenty-first century, the Mint Question is moot. Hypersweetened iced tea and **Coca-Cola** have taken the Mint Julep's place as the Grits Belt's summer cooler of choice. It matters as much to the vast majority of Southern manhood—and everyone else—as whether the Holy Spirit proceeds from the Father to the Son or the Father and the Son (the famous 'filioque' debate that so exercised medieval theologians).

Ecumenical to the quick, we'll take our communion from either school without scruple.

JULEP #1—UN-MUDDLED

(Representing the Lowland or Pendennis School of Julepistics)

Use a 14-oz or 16-oz silver julep cup

Dissolve 1 lump (or less) of granulated sugar in a splash of clear spring water

Add 2 or 3 sprigs of tender mint, place gently—don't bruise the mint

Fill the cup with cracked ice

Add a generous 3 oz of Kentucky bourbon whiskey

Stir gently and refill the julep cup with cracked ice

Take a full bunch of tender mint, cutting the ends to bleed, and place on top

Let it stand for about 5 minutes before serving.

JULEP #2— MUDDLED

(Representing the High Kentucky School of Julepistics)

Place 5 or 6 leaves of mint in the bottom of a pre-chilled, dry 12-oz glass or silver beaker

Add 1 teaspoon sugar and crush slightly with a muddler

Pack glass with finely cracked ice

Pour a generous 3 oz of Kentucky bourbon over the ice

Stir briskly until the glass frosts

Add more ice and stir again before serving

Stick a few sprigs of mint into the ice so that the partaker will get the aroma

Still not enough mint flavor? Try this: for each Julep, lightly cover about 10 sprigs of mint with bar sugar, add an ounce of spring water, macerate, let stand for 10 to 15 minutes, and strain through a fine sieve into the ice-filled glass. Then add whiskey and proceed as above. If you'll stoop to maceration, you might also want to float ½ oz of dark Jamaica rum on top.

▲ **Priestly vestments of the Julep cult, late-twentieth century.**

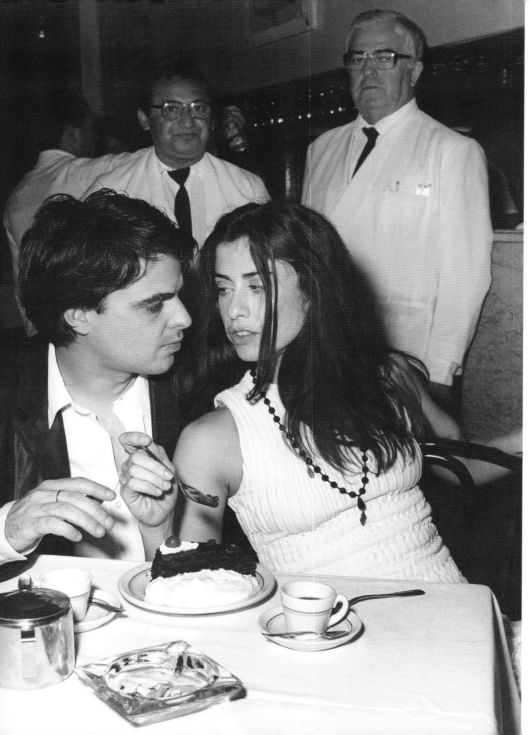

Paolo: *E poi?*
Francesca: *Dai, Paolo—*
il Stinger.

THE FIRST & THE LAST

Apéritifs & After-Dinner Drinks

ON THE **CONTINENT** (the European one, that is), they drink differently than we do. Not always worse, but differently. Their drinks tend to be lighter on the firewater, heavier on the herbal bitter and liqueur.

Fine drinks, as long as your craving for a cocktail is more psychological than physical. But they definitely eat better than we do, and all those botanicals, they claim, stimulate the appetite. We've accepted that claim at face value, and lumped the Continental-style appetite-inciter together here in the food section with those sweet, heavy things you take to sit on a big meal. Oh, and the hot ones you serve in a mug (we can't remember precisely why those are here, but we're too stuffed to ask 'em to move).

THE APÉRITIF

AMERICANO

Campari Soda, **Negroni**, Americano—the holy trinity of Italian mixology. This one, they say, got its name from the extraordinary amount of Campari Americans were putting away during Prohibition. Campari, you see, was *legal* in the States: it was a digestive bitter—a medicine—not a recreational bevvy. A 48-proof digestive bitter, we should point out. (And that still doesn't explain the vermouth.) Could we have made it from 1919 to 1933 on these alone? If those years consisted entirely of lazy summer afternoons, you bet.

BAMBOO

Credited to bartender Charlie Mahoney of the Hoffman House, Manhattan, this most elegant of apéritif-cocktails was supposedly named after Bob Cole's hit song, "Under the Bamboo Tree." 'Credited.' 'Supposedly.' Bartenders are not historians, and all too few historians are barflies—if the unacceptable laxness with which the annals of drink have been compiled is any sign.

If the drink is in fact Mahoney's mixological comment on Cole, that would date its creation to 1902, when the song was published, or soon after. And Cole (1868-1911) certainly deserved a drink, not only for his own efforts—he was one of the pioneers of the Black musical theater—but for his impeccable taste in associates. His usual writing partner was J. Rosamond Johnson, who, with his brother James Weldon Johnson, wrote "Lift Ev'ry Voice and Sing," called by many the Black national anthem.

VARIANTS & MIXOLOGY

With Italian vermouth instead of French (and a twist of orange peel instead of the olive), it's either an **Adonis**, so named in honor of Henry Dixey's 1884 theatrical smash (the first Broadway musical), or—if you prefer your ham canned—an **Armour**, after the pig-packer.

AMERICANO

Pour 1½ oz Italian vermouth and 1½ oz Campari into an ice-filled Collins glass and top off with soda

Garnish with slice of orange or lemon.

BAMBOO

Stir well with cracked ice:

2 oz dry sherry

2 oz French vermouth

2 dashes orange bitters

Strain into chilled cocktail glass

Garnish, if you wish, with an olive.

CAMPARI SODA

Pour 3 oz Campari into a Collins glass with 2 or 3 ice cubes in it and top off with soda

Garnish with slice of lemon or orange.

VARIANTS & MIXOLOGY

If you use orange juice instead of soda, that's called a **Garibaldi**, which is as pleasant a way of absorbing your Vitamin C as any we know.

DUBONNET COCKTAIL

Stir well with cracked ice:

1½ oz London dry gin

1½ oz red Dubonnet

Strain into chilled cocktail glass and garnish with lemon slice. (Whiskey, sherry, vermouth or rum may be used in place of gin; the combinations are legion.)

VARIANTS & MIXOLOGY

If making a **Rum Dubonnet**, use the golden Puerto Rican variety, and add the juice of one-half lime; shake and strain.

CAMPARI SODA

You're sitting on one of those woven lanyard-plastic chairs under a *caffè* umbrella in the piazza in the middle of town, watching mothers and their impossibly beautiful teenage daughters stroll arm-in-arm past the *duomo* as they eat their gelato in the late-afternoon sun. Here's your *cameriere*. "*Buona sera, signore.*" "Campari Soda, *per favore.*" Right now, right here, life is good.

DUBONNET COCKTAIL

"On the corner of Fifth Avenue and Twenty-sixth Street, close to where the bronze Diana stands, poised against the blue, is the Café Martin, where the Dry Martini is more palely golden than anywhere else on the Isle, where the people are more attractive and all the delights more bewitchingly treacherous." So Mary MacLane (who had astounded the world by publishing an accomplished and racy autobiography at age 19), in 1910.

In 1899, when Delmonico's (see the **Delmonico Number 1**) cleared out of their Madison Square location, a certain Louis Martin snapped it up and decorated it in the new style he'd picked up while touring France—Art Nouveau. What's more, he boldly decreed that his joint would be, as Miss MacLane put it, "cordial in its welcome to unescorted women." Result: every daring young thing in town—in the country (Mary MacLane, for instance, was from Butte)—simply *had* to go there. There was really nowhere else in America a lady could drink, in public.

Café Martin's **Martinis** were no doubt delightful, but the real mixological action there involved Dubonnet—the quinine-laced, winelike substance you still see advertised all over France. Just the thing to feature at his new café, Martin figured, so he began importing it. Of course, the ladies, gentle, fair, weaker sex and all, were still Americans, dammit, and they liked their Dubonnet with some backbone. Hence the Dubonnet Cocktail, a potion quite unknown in France but all the rage where folks liked their delights with an edge of bewitching treachery to them (you can only *just* taste the gin).

NEGRONI

The Italians, as a rule, are not drinkers—at least, not as the Anglo-Saxon understands the term. A single Australian could drink a roomful of 'em stinkibus and still drive down to the pub for a nightcap. It's not that they avoid the stuff; they just don't consider it sufficient recreation unto itself. Alcohol goes *with* things.

As a result, the Italian boot is some of the sorriest cocktail country in Christendom. The national liquor—*grappa*—is, by and large, frightful, unless you're willing to disburse astronomical sums for it; gummy, sweet liqueurs abound, and nobody knows how to make a dry **Martini**. Luckily, there's Campari.

Campari has associations. Summer-weight suits with narrow lapels, Ray-Ban Wayfarers, Vespas, brown-eyed blondes in Capri pants. *La dolce vita*. A violently red, bittered-up, 48-proof apéritif doesn't sound like much to build a cocktail culture on, but somehow it works. In fact, when you team it up with gin and the local vermouth, you get one of the world's indispensable cocktails. (Accounts differ as to who this Negroni person was, but—as the **Camparinete**—the drink itself goes back to at least 1934; some give time and place of origin as Florence, 1920, but the jury's still out.)

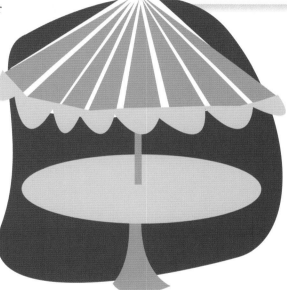

NEGRONI

Stir well with cracked ice:

1½ oz London dry gin

1 oz Campari

1 oz Italian vermouth

Strain into chilled cocktail glass and garnish with twist of orange peel.

SHERRY COCKTAIL

This is the kind of thing your maiden aunt produces on those rare occasions when she entertains her sibling's grown children—provided, of course, she's the kind of maiden aunt whose spinsterhood is the result of too many suitors, not too few. And rich ones, at that—Europeans, mostly. You always did think she was cool.

SHERRY COCKTAIL

Mix:

2 oz dry sherry, pre-chilled

2 oz French vermouth, pre-chilled

Serve with ice in a small highball glass or goblet.

VERMOUTH CASSIS

Pour 3 oz French vermouth and ½ oz crème de cassis into a Collins glass

Add 2 or 3 ice cubes and top off with club soda or seltzer to taste.

Note: Some authorities insist that a true Pompier is in fact made not with crème de cassis—a low-proof, sticky liqueur made from black currants—but with strawberry syrup. That may be so, but we like it fine this way. Authenticity is a good thing only until it forces you to do book research on the drinking habits of pre-World War I French firemen. And besides, strawberry syrup? Nah.

VERMOUTH CASSIS

This traditional French tipple, a.k.a. the **Pompier** (French for 'fireman'), was quite the rage over here in the 1930s, especially with types who had the leisure and the inclination to while away the idle hours in the pseudo-Parisian sidewalk cafés of Manhattan, exchanging world-weary observations with handsome and moneyed members of the opposite sex (or, truth be told, the same sex—does it really matter?).

While we're sure that Café Society back then was just as blithering as its modern equivalent, we have to admit it got one thing right. Although perhaps not the best drink to order in the company of Anglo-Saxons or hard drinkers of any stripe (okay, Russians), the Vermouth Cassis is in fact one of the most refreshing and elegant summer drinks going. We have more to learn from the celebutant(e) than how to tie a cravat or carry a yip-dog, it turns out. The two-fisted drinker doesn't know everything.

AFTER DINNER, COLD

BRANDY ALEXANDER

BRANDY ALEXANDER

Shake well with cracked ice:

1 oz brandy

1 oz crème de cacao

1 oz heavy cream

Strain into chilled cocktail glass.

As a rule, we have eschewed the autobiographical mode in these pages, writing about oneself being as plaguy an activity these days as bunging what-have-you into a conical glass and calling it a **Martini**. But the circumstances under which we came to know the Brandy Alexander have forever colored our perception of the drink.

At the beginning of the 1980s, Midtown Manhattan was home to an ungodly number of so-called 'stress clinics', where one could, after pretend-ing to see a doctor, obtain a prescription for Quaaludes, which are still con-sidered by many to be the Dom Perignon of pharmaceutics. One would then take this precious piece of paper—it would generally set you back about $125—to a pharmacy, but not just any pharmacy: most druggists, noting the extraordinary number of scrips that Dr. Quispiam (an alias; please don't sue) was writing, would drop a dime on him post haste. A select few, however, were happy to fork over the gow, no questions asked (kickbacks? you bet).

At the time, we—all right, fine, *I*—worked for a certain criminal lawyer, who represented one of these druggists. I was the legs of the operation.

Now for the Brandy Alexanders: a couple of days after I start, my boss (a former judge, no less) sends me over to this guy's pharmacy, to pick up his personal 'lude prescription (lower-back pain, I think he said it was). Mr. Jackson, let's call him, is supposed to have it all ready for me, in a little bag. I get there, and of course, no Mr. Jackson. If I can stick around…? I can. The stockboy pops out the door. A minute or two later, he's back. But no Mr. Jackson. Finally, eventually, a guy in a stained lab-coat rolls in: three hundred pounds, bald with a greasy fringe, face like yesterday's oatmeal, short a couple of fingers on one hand. Half in the bag, too. Mr. Jackson.

Next time, the time after: same thing. Finally I get wise: there's an O'Chumley's, whatever, next door to the pharmacy; before letting another

VARIANTS & MIXOLOGY

The Brandy Alexander, formerly known as the **Panama** and the **Alexander Number 2**, is an adaptation (attributed to Harry MacElhone of Harry's New York Bar, Paris) of the **Alexander**, which is based on gin rather than brandy. It's kinda disgusting, but it is the original. (Both species were particularly popular during Prohibition, since the cream and the chocolate would go a ways towards muffling the taste of the rotgut you built 'em on.)

half-hour die among the laxatives and cut-rate cosmetics, I figure I'll just pop my head in the bar. Sure enough, there's Jackson, sucking down something brownish and creamy out of a little cocktail glass. Three empties in front of him. It's 11:30 in the morning. I go over to him. "Hey, lookee here. The Judge's kid. Must want his candy." Wave of the arm in the general direction of the bartender. "Get the kid a Brandy Alexander."

They stopped making Quaaludes and I don't know what became of Mr. Jackson, but to this day I—we—don't drink Brandy Alexanders. But don't let that stop you.

CAFÉ COCKTAIL

Shake well with cracked ice:

1 oz brandy

1 oz crème de cacao

2 oz black coffee

1 teaspoon bar sugar

Strain into chilled cocktail glass and garnish with twist of lemon peel.

CAFÉ COCKTAIL

Murdock Pemberton collected this for our February, 1939 "Potables" column; we think it hails from the Floridita bar in Havana, and we know it's delicious (if you like 'em on the sweet side).

COMMODORE

A favorite punching-bag of serious mixologists has long been the ladies' drink: that sweet, fruity, un-liquorly concoction that comes loaded with things like cream and egg white and a considerable charge of well-disguised inhibition- (and therefore, the theory goes, undergarment-) remover. "If the girl does not like it, do not drink it, but pour it quickly into the nearest flower vase," the 1930 *Savoy Cocktail Book* advises. The names don't help: **Pink Lady**, Poet's Dream, **Maiden's Prayer**. Manly.

Yet to survey the fine art of mixing drinks as it is practiced today is to appreciate the crushing totality of the ladies' drink's conquest. And it's not just the **Cosmopolitan** we're talking about. Anything with banana liqueur, melon, strawberry, chocolate—ladies' drink. Anything with more liqueur than liquor—ladies' drink. Anything with cranberry juice—borderline, we're afraid. Taken together, all those account for a frighteningly high percentage of new cocktails.

But so what? Tastes change, and the new drinker seems to like 'em sweet. That's happened before: take the Commodore. Crème de cacao, grenadine, bourbon…sounds like something cooked up for the 1996 World Cocktail Championships (no, really—such things exist) by Jimbo the bartender at Rick's Yabbie Shack, Bondi Beach, Australia. Nix. The original is to be found in the venerable Waldorf-Astoria bar book, from pre-Prohibition days. In fact, many a drink from the golden age of the cocktail (when bars were strictly men-only) is about as butch as Liberace in lace panties. So hold your head high and repeat after us: "I love the Commodore." Why? Because it's damn tasty. And it's just a drink.

GYPSY

From the hand-cranked era of vodka drinks. We present the Gypsy—a.k.a. the **Vodka Queen**—not so much for its historical interest, which is slight, but because this is an excellent way of drinking liqueur: you get all the flavor, while the vodka cuts the stickiness and lightens the body. The recipe dates back to 1935.

COMMODORE

Shake well with cracked ice:

1½ oz bourbon

1 oz crème de cacao (white, preferably)

1 oz lemon juice

Dash of grenadine

Strain into chilled champagne glass.

Alternatively, this one makes a good blender drink: just add four or five ice cubes per drink and whir it up.

GYPSY

Shake well with cracked ice:

2 oz vodka

1 oz Bénédictine

Dash of Angostura bitters

Strain into chilled cocktail glass.

MILLIONAIRE

"Shake with cracked ice as though 7 demons were goading you to it" (Mackall):

2 oz rye whiskey (actually, here's where Canadian Club might be more appropriate—that being what Brits back then thought of when they thought of North American whiskey)

½ oz orange curaçao

Dash of grenadine

White of 1 egg

Strain into chilled cocktail glass.

MILLIONAIRE

Drinking is 'aspirational', to use the buzz-word current in magazine circles for 'reading about things that you'll never be able to afford or are too chicken to do.' Thus single-malt Scotch stands in for that grouse-range in Scotland, Rebel Yell bourbon the pole position at Daytona, and so forth. That's not the whole story, of course: there's the element of taste—the physical sense, not the sense of style—and, of course, the problem of ignorance (how else do you explain Tequiza?). But, deny it as you will, a significant factor in your choice of what to drink is whether or not you think it makes you look cool.

The typical millionaire, circa 1920: top hat, tails, sweep-fendered Rolls Royce, the whole Scrooge McDuck bit. An image with traction. In fact, it spawned several cocktails of that name, none of which a true millionaire would order. It was bad enough that these formulae wore their aspirations on their sleeves— back then, in the age before Trump with a capital T, a millionaire had to at least pretend that it wasn't all about the Benjamins. Worse, though, most of 'em sucked. But here's one—credited to the Ritz Hotel in London, sometime before 1925—that "tastes sense," as Lawton Mackall put it in our October, 1940 "Potables" column. Sweet, pleasant, even jovial. In fact, judging from actual millionaires we have met, rather atypical.

NETHERLAND

Back in the Golden Age of the American saloon, before the farmers and haberdashers and other dry what-have-yous looked to the law to stop what they couldn't by moral example, a bartender had to be a craftsman, an adept in the alchemical arts who could perfectly reproduce a thousand and one potions without consulting any formulary but the one in his head—right? Wrong. As old-time newspaperman George Ade observed, "to serve drinks in the common run of places required no more technical skill than is needed to put food in front of domestic animals." In most saloons, if you ordered a cocktail—any cocktail, not just a Bunny Hug or a Fluffy Ruffles—you'd get the fisheye. If you persisted, the boot. Whiskey—plain—was good enough for most drinking men, with or without a schooner of beer on the side.

Now, true adepts did exist, but you had to know where to find them. Your best bet was always the bar in a big-city hotel, and not a cheap one. And naturally, New York, the biggest and most expensive city, had the most. The Cosmopolitan (after which the current drink was most assuredly *not* named), the Broadway Central, the Brevoort, the St. Denis, the Everett House, the Continental, the Fifth Avenue, and on and on into the dozens—all maintained meticulous bars, oases of oak and cut glass where you could order anything from an **Amsterdam** to a **Woxum** (that's an ounce of applejack, an ounce of Italian vermouth and half an ounce of yellow Chartreuse) and be assured of perfection in the result.

Just about every one of these palais de hooch had a house cocktail, needless to say. A few of them survived the Volstead act, including the potent **Waldorf**, the **Hoffman House** (a **Martini** with orange bitters; recommended), the Holland House (a **Martini** with fruit; not recommended)—and the Netherland. Although the New Netherland Hotel, on Fifth Avenue at Fifty-ninth Street, was for a time the tallest in the world, its signature drink is a modest affair: just a splash of brandy, a dash of curaçao, a drop or two of orange bitters. Still, there is elegance here. Brandy and bitter orange enjoy a relationship based on mutual esteem and sympathy, feelings that they will impart to you and that delightful someone as you sip your Netherlands. After dinner, preferably—the drink is on the sweet side. But, ahem, so are you, right?

NETHERLAND

Stir well with cracked ice:

2 oz brandy

⅔ oz orange curaçao (or less—individual taste must decide)

Dash of orange bitters

Strain into chilled cocktail glass.

VARIANTS & MIXOLOGY

Add a dash of Absinthe or legal (or illegal) substitute and you've got a **Dream**.

QUEEN ELIZABETH

Shake well with cracked ice:

2 oz French vermouth

1 oz Bénédictine

1 oz lime juice

Strain into chilled cocktail glass.

Note: Should you plan to palm this off on an Anglo-Saxon, it would be wise to serve a glass of hooch on the side.

QUEEN ELIZABETH

A French drink, according to Lawton Mackall, writing in our October, 1939 "Potables" column. Fair enough. But why does he label it a "happy heresy"? Is it because it's named after a Queen of England (the first of that name, since the second was still a mere Princess), yet has nothing English in it? Or is it because there were already two cocktails of that name in the standard bar books, neither anything like this one? No matter; those were rather pedestrian affairs. Not this. A little too sweet for before-dinner tippling, to be sure, but *après*? The herbal notes of the Bénédictine and the vermouth are balanced by the liqueur's sweetness and the lime juice's delicate acidity. The French school of mixology has its moments.

◀ (News flash: information has just reached us that the Q.E. was in fact spawned by a 1935 U.S. cocktail contest, which it won. What do we know?)

SAM WARD

After-dinner drinking is, as we all know, a minefield. Well, it is in polite company, anyway. You crack open the cognac, put it there on the table, and next thing you know, Melinda's on her third and doesn't care who knows it, Paolo's spilling things down his front, and Frank and Phil are taking their differences regarding the films of Jill Clayburgh just a little too seriously. On the other hand, withhold it and you're a cheapskate.

The prudent host has traditionally had recourse to the liqueur, a class of liquid asset so sweet that only the truly desperate drinker can wade through more than one. Problem is, even the most mild-mannered folks can turn desperate on you in the throes of after-dinner chitchat. Bottles die. Kung fu ensues. The only solution is to give them one drink, but with just enough ritual that they'll be embarrassed to make you produce another.

Enter Sam Ward.

Old Sam Ward was one of the early sachems of the New York Stock Exchange. But, since he was also the first president of the New-York City Temperance Society, we're not going to talk about him. We're going to talk about Sam Ward the Younger, his son. Here's Walter Barrett, from his *Old Merchants of New York City* (1862): "His son married one of the Astor girls, and has plenty of money, keeps fast horses, is a sort of diplomat, and a very good fellow."

Sure, Junior had his ups and downs—fortunes lost, fortunes won again, that sort of thing—but throughout it all, he remained a good fellow at heart (he even tried to get Oscar Wilde a guest membership to his club; not a chance). And if the Astors dropped him after Emily—his Astor wife—died (or maybe it was because he was temporarily insolvent), even they had to admit he knew how to eat and what to drink while he was doing it. Did he invent the Sam Ward? History is silent. Still, it's an old drink, going back to the Manhattan Club (see the **Manhattan**), and a surprisingly good one: the residual lemon juice cuts the sweetness of the Chartreuse, the ice does what ice does, and it looks cool.

SAM WARD

Remove the innards from half a lemon (a grapefruit knife makes this a snap)

Tuck it into a small cocktail glass—or just shave a little off the bottom so it'll stand up—and pack it with shaved ice

Fill with yellow Chartreuse and serve (green Chartreuse will work as well, but it's 110 proof—do you really want to go there?) Apricot brandy—the dry Hungarian variety—is also traditional.

SGROPPINO

Blend 1 oz vodka, 1½ oz lemon sorbet and 2 oz finely crushed ice for 20 seconds on high

Serve in a champagne flute.

STINGER

Stir well with cracked ice:

2 oz brandy

1 oz white crème de menthe (⅔ oz is even better)

Strain into chilled cocktail glass. The Stinger is sometimes served with a pair of short straws.

VARIANTS & MIXOLOGY

If you go with ⅔ oz crème de menthe and drop in a dash of Angostura and a twist of lemon peel, that's a **Brant**. And don't tell anyone we said so, but the Stinger is just as tasty if you make it with a good white rum, such as Brugal.

SGROPPINO

A *sgroppino*—roughly, 'little un-knotter'—is what they serve you in the northeastern regions of Italy after you've stuffed yourself like a mortadella. Usually, it relies on *prosecco*, the local bubbly, for its alcoholic kick. Sometimes, though, that's just not enough. We encountered this jumped-up version at the Antica Trattoria Suban, in the hills above Trieste. We needed it: Suban specializes in the cuisine of the old Austro-Hungarian Empire, who used to run things in those parts. After dining there, we can understand why the Empire collapsed. They were just too full to move. If they had had the Sgroppino, who knows?

STINGER

"Stingers, and keep them coming"—Cary Grant, as Navy pilot, in 'Kiss Them for Me' (check out Jayne Mansfield in this one—talk about stingers!). In fact, our 1949 *Handbook for Hosts* identifies the Stinger as a favorite with flyboys back in the Big One—whether it's because they were a bunch of college boys who hadn't got used to the taste of real liquor or because of the mint oil's well-known property of disguising the alcohol on one's breath. In any case, it's as quick a way to fill up on the old C_2H_5OH as any known.

The Stinger's origins are obscure. Pre-Prohibition, sure—it turns up, for instance, in Tom Bullock's 1917 *Ideal Bartender*—but beyond that, we're stumped. Traditionally, it was strictly an after-dinner drink. But then, some time in the mid 1920s, Reginald Vanderbilt (father of little Gloria) took to moistening the clay with them before his meals at New York's celeb-infested The Colony. In a lesser name, that would of course be considered vulgar. But if a Vanderbilt's doing it, it must be kosher. Stingers all around.

AFTER DINNER, HOT
(plus a couple of anytime warmers)

Café Grog

When leaves turn sere and wither on the branch and chill-fingered Canadian winds pry into all our carelessly guarded nooks and crannies, we can't feel a damned thing. We've taken the precaution, you see, of upholstering our vitals with a thick layer of Café Grog. There are times when nothing else will serve. Whenever the Fahrenheit's looking at twenty from the south side, it's time. Whenever tiny old ladies venture abroad only at the risk of becoming thickly bundled windborne projectiles, it's time. And whenever we've got a houseful of nice folks who come bearing gifts and claims that we're somehow related, it's *definitely* time.

Café Grog is simple, tasty, and not unlike a speedball in its effect, especially if you've got a really good espresso machine.

Metaphorical representation of Café Grog in action. ▶

CAFÉ GROG

In a small saucepan, mix:

1 oz dark Jamaica rum

½ oz brandy

2 lumps of sugar

1 slice lemon

4 oz black coffee

Heat until simmering and serve immediately.

HOT BUTTERED RUM

In a mug, dissolve 1 or 2 lumps of sugar in a little hot water and add:

2 oz dark Jamaica rum—or Medford rum, should such a thing still exist

Pat of unsalted butter (about ½ tablespoon)

Fill the mug with hot water and sprinkle a little nutmeg on top, if you feel the calling (we generally take ours without).

You can also substitute cider for the water and add a ½ teaspoon of mixed cinnamon and cloves, but that's getting away from the rock-ribbed simplicity of the thing. If you're a real purist, you'll put everything in a mug and then ram a red-hot poker into it until it steams—a most satisfying operation, but not to be considered after round three.

HOT BUTTERED RUM

In 1860, the United States is a nation divided against itself. In the South, a man will do or die for corn whiskey (unless he's a plantation-owner or other member of the oppressor class; see the **Jubal Early Punch**). In Delaware, Maryland, Pennsylvania and New York, it's rye that stokes the furnace. New Jersey swears by applejack, New Orleans, brandy; out West—well, they'll drink pretty much anything. That leaves Ohio and the new states of the Midwest, who are doing their damnedest to eliminate the stuff altogether, and old New England.

There, it's rum, rum and more rum. Now, when we think of distilling sugarcane, we think of places with names like 'Montego Bay', 'Havana', 'Anguilla', 'Martinique', 'Bahia'—like that. Not 'Medford', 'Pawtucket', 'Salem' or 'Boston.' Fact is, they used to make a hell of a lot of the stuff up there, and sell it all over the place. This is a drink essay, so we're not gonna get into the brutal facts of the Triangle Trade (look it up), but trust us, the Yankees didn't come by the biz honestly. There were slaves involved.

At any rate, they drank rum hot. They drank it cold. They drank it straight. They drank it mixed—with water, lemon juice, orange juice, apple juice, baked apple; sugar (always sugar), maple sugar, maple syrup, molasses; brandy, gin, ale, port, Madeira; nutmeg, cloves and all the Christmas spices; egg whites, egg yolks, whole eggs, milk, cream, butter, just about everything this side of whale oil (although…nah). And when the local industry faded away (the abolition of the slave trade put a serious crimp in it, and Prohibition more or less finished it) and the folks in New England began to guzzle whiskey and dry **Martinis** just like everybody else, they still hung on to rum for medicinal purposes.

This particular compound is indicated for *digitipedum glaciati*, or, in the vulgate, 'frozen tootsies', an affliction for which it is often prescribed (age being no barrier, we might add, over ninety and under ten included) to be taken prophylactically or preventatively throughout the colder parts of the year—which, in New England, run roughly from August to June.

Oh yeah, the purpose of the butter? According the 1939 *Gun Club Drink Book*, it's only there to lubricate your mustache. Good enough.

Irish Coffee

You would think that it would be impossible to be unhappy while sipping an Irish Coffee. Yet, seated at the bar, we've noticed far too many times that the face behind the traditional stemmed glass mug is tinged with sadness. Drink can be a comfort, at times, but even a warm, generous drink such as this can prove to be a cold consolation. We sip the promising cup in hope, but things are not better. In our mouths, yes. In our innards, aglow, yes. Even in our veins. In our hearts? No. Go home.

A note on origin: Irish Coffee was born in 1942 at a tiny flying boat terminal in Foynes, Ireland (on the River Shannon), when a cook by the name of Joe Sheridan threw it together for some passengers for Newfoundland who had just spent ten hours in the air getting precisely nowhere, since their flight turned back in the mid-Atlantic due to bad weather. They, at least, must've been comforted.

IRISH COFFEE

Pour into stemmed glass mug:

2 oz Irish whisky (John Power's is traditional)

6 oz hot black coffee

Sugar to taste

Top off with lightly whipped heavy cream. If too lazy or inebriated or depressed to bother whipping the stuff, just pour 1 to 2 oz in over the back of a spoon.

Irish Whiskey Skin

"[Whiskey] doesn't sustain life, but, whin taken hot with wather, a lump iv sugar, a piece iv lemon peel, and just th' dustin' iv a nutmeg-grater, it makes life sustainable." So Finley Peter Dunne, the Chicago-Irish humorist of the 1890s. Judging from the drink he contributed to *So Red the Nose*, a 1935 anthology of writers' drinks, *Esquire*'s founding editor Arnold Gingrich was of the same opinion. **Esky's Hot Spot**, as he called it, was identical with the drink Mr. Dunne described—which is merely the venerable Irish Whiskey Skin, as described in 1862 by Professor Jerry Thomas of **Tom and Jerry** fame.

Not the drink you'd expect from an urbane sophisticate like Gingrich. But, like Dunne, he was based in Chicago. You know what the weather's like there.

IRISH WHISKEY SKIN

Put a lump of sugar (½ teaspoon) and a short strip of lemon peel in a mug, add 2 oz Irish whiskey and about 4 oz boiling water.

Dust with nutmeg, if you like.

PUNCH LIVORNESE

In a shot glass, muddle ½ teaspoon sugar and a 1-inch twist of lemon peel in ½ oz brandy.

Top up with espresso, as strong, dark and hot as you can make it (an espresso machine is essential; drip coffee just won't do it).

Also indicated for: depression, grippe, fatigue and existential angst.

PUNCH LIVORNESE

Leghorn—Livorno, to the natives—is a gritty port on the Tuscan coast without much to recommend it to the tourist. Unless you like to eat seafood. The Livornese approach cooking fish like hand-to-hand combat, a desperate knife-edge struggle for mastery with no quarter offered and none accepted. *Cacciucco*, their version of a bouillabaisse, is one result: a primordial stew of tentacles, sea-flesh, nameless shelly things, saffron, tomatoes and chili pepper that, if ingested at lunch, will render you quadriplegic for the rest of the day should you fail to immediately down a couple of these.

RULE #812

Grownups do not drink shooters— not even for 'research'.

The economies of
scale. Just don't
drink it all at once.

THE FLOWING BOWL

Punches, Tropical & Arctic

WHO THE HELL WANTS TO MIX DRINKS? You've got a couple dozen deeply interesting individuals meandering through the back forty (or milling around the living room), talking about deeply interesting things—money, sex, real estate—and here you are messing with ice, glasses and bottles whose caps you keep misplacing. One word: Punch.

We know punch (a Hindi word, it turns out; the Brits discovered the stuff in India, back in the 1600s) seems kinda old fashioned, but if made right—not too sweet, too fussy or too weak—it'll really give a party the boot in the ass it sometimes needs to get going. And you can actually talk to people.

There are almost as many punches as there are people who mix 'em; this is the most improvisational area of mixology. Here are a select few classics, both Tropical—hot weather, in other words—and Arctic—cold weather. Most of the following recipes will make up one large bowl. How many people that serves depends upon the company you keep. Whatever you do, though, try to avoid those tiny little glass punch-cups known as 'knuckle-traps.' To use them, as Lawton Mackall observed, is to ladle the sublime into the ridiculous.

PUNCHES, TROPICAL

ARISTOCRAT SPARKLING PUNCH

According to our February, 1942 "Potables" column, this is what they were solacing their existences with out on Catalina Island, the swank resort that hovers just far enough off the coast of Los Angeles to escape the smog, but not so far that you can't see the searchlights. That 'Aristocrat'? Wishful thinking, unless you're okay with the phrase 'movie royalty.'

The Hollywood sign.

ARISTOCRAT SPARKLING PUNCH

2 bottles brut champagne

1 bottle burgundy (at the time, this would've been California burgundy, but we prefer a decent Côtes du Rhone)

4 oz brandy

1 cup bar sugar

1 liter sparkling water

Dissolve the sugar in a cup of the sparkling water and pour it into a punch bowl

Add the 'burgundy' and the brandy, stirring well

Place a block of ice in the bowl and add the champagne and the balance of the sparkling water

Decorate the top of the ice block with strawberries or raspberries, or other fruit in season, and float thin slices of two oranges on top of the punch.

BRANDY PUNCH

Assemble:

1 cup orange curaçao (for slightly higher voltage, use Cointreau or—go for broke!—Grand Marnier)

½ oz grenadine (optional)

4 oz orange juice

1 cup lemon juice

1 cup bar sugar (or less—the curaçao is plenty sweet)

1 quart brandy

1 liter sparkling water

Mix the curaçao, the grenadine and the fruit juices, check for sweetness, and stir in sugar to taste until it has dissolved

Add the brandy and let sit for a while in a cool place

When the hour of hospitality is at hand, pour into a punch bowl over a large piece of ice and add the sparkling water

Garnish, if you wish, with thin wheels of lemon.

BRANDY PUNCH

This recipe is a perfect example of where punchistics stood in the middle of the nineteenth century, when the science of compounding punches was at—or perhaps a little past—its peak. The recipe is, taken all in all, strong, simple, elegant and very effective (although we cannot help but regard the addition of grenadine, no matter how small the quantity, as a sign of incipient decadence). Beyond that, little needs to be said. Which is good, since we haven't a clue where this recipe, printed in our 1949 *Handbook for Hosts*, actually came from. So build away and have at it, blissfully untroubled by pesky thoughts of men and events long-past.

CHAMPAGNE PUNCH

There was a time when you couldn't graduate from State, kiss a bride, make a first million or snip off a foreskin without toasting it in Champagne Punch. And why not? This is one old dame who's still got a little life in 'er.

The varieties of Champagne Punch are as many as the causes of human jubilation, ranging all the way from pure champagne poured over ice and decorated with a few lemon slices to a concoction stepped up with half the contents of a good liquor cabinet and stretched out with the mingled essences of a California fruit-stand. We like this one for its moderation.

CLARET CUP

According to the 1869 *Cups and Their Customs*, by Henry Porter and George Roberts, the Claret Cup is "the most agreeable, wholesome, [and] easily compounded" of wine punches. They weren't wrong. Dryer and less cloying than Sangria, more robust than its cousin the **White Wine Cup**, a good Claret Cup will perk up an afternoon affair without causing unseemly revelry. Perfect, in short, for the kind of shindig where you've got folks of all ages, some of whom might be in a position to make your life rather difficult should you indulge your natural desire to get 'faced and demonstrate the proper way to do the Dirty Boogie.

CHAMPAGNE PUNCH

To each bottle of brut add:

1½ oz brandy

1½ oz Cointreau

1 liter club soda

Rind of one orange, cut very thin

Little or no bar sugar and no lemon

Then add as big a berg of ice as you can produce, decorate with sliced fresh pineapple and orange, and plenty of fresh mint.

CLARET CUP

Mix in large bowl:

1 bottle decent, but not lavish, Bordeaux

4 oz Amontillado or cream sherry

2 oz maraschino (or 1 oz brandy and 1 oz orange curaçao)

Rind of 1 lemon, cut very thin

Bar sugar to taste (1 oz or less)

1 liter club soda

"Let stand an hour or so for inter-jubilation of ingredients," as our Lawton Mackall advised back in 1939. Deposit berg of ice, pour in the chilled club soda and deck out with pineapple and orange slices, fresh mint or a curl of fresh cucumber rind.

FISH HOUSE PUNCH

2 quarts dark Jamaica rum

1 quart cognac

4 oz peach brandy—not a drop more; the stuff penetrates (Hiram Walker makes an acceptable version, as long as you don't sip it straight; whatever you do, don't use peach schnapps—even Southern Comfort would be better.)

1 quart lemon juice

¾ lb (1½ cups) bar sugar

2 quarts spring water (all right, tap water)

In a large bowl, first dissolve the sugar in enough of the water to do the trick, then incorporate the lemon juice

Next, add the spirits and the rest of the water—or as much of it as you wish to contribute (less in summer, to allow for meltage)

Slip in the proverbial berg of ice (use your imagination—a mixing bowl full of water and frozen overnight will do the trick; run a little hot water on the outside of the bowl to unmold)

Let stand in a cool place for an hour or so before serving.

FISH HOUSE PUNCH

Philadelphia in July. The City of Brotherly Love being at roughly the same latitude as Naples and sharing its summer climate, you will sweat. A lot. Especially if it's 1776, and you've been sitting all day in the States House (soon to be renamed Independence Hall), with air conditioning a century and a half away. But all is not lost: there is Fish House Punch.

Back in 1732, a selection of Philly bigwigs had ganged together to start a club; they called it, for reasons best known unto them, the State in Schuylkill Fishing Corporation. They built themselves a house on the banks of the 'Skookul', as it's pronounced, concocted themselves an official punch, and set to it. Fish. Drink. Eat. (The club's still around, so they must have been doing something right.)

Their punch caught on, pretty much right away, and small wonder: this refreshing tipple is so tasty that you'll want to stick away about a quart of it and so strong that you'll soon forget where your pants are—even if you happen to still be wearing them, which is by no means certain. But we digress.

Until you've tried Fish House Punch, you can't possibly understand what burdens the Founding Fathers labored under as they sat there figuring out how to get us out from under King George's size-twelves. Knowing what we do about early American drinking habits—in 1792, fewer than 4,000,000 Americans sopped up over 11,000,000 gallons of liquor alone—we can't imagine that the delegates kept the stuff at arm's length. So, if they were anything at all like us, they would have had to be drunk. Blotto. Absolutely embalmed. But they weren't like us, were they?

Naples-on-the-Schuylkill. ▼

JUBAL EARLY PUNCH

What? No bourbon? You'd imagine a punch named after a Confederate general would have at least a *little* of the stuff in it. We've got a theory (don't we always?). Jubal Anderson Early was a gentleman of the antebellum South, and true Southern gentlemen generally left whiskey for Yankees and other representatives of the classless society. Given their druthers, they drank imported. The war changed all that, of course—all the Rhett Butlers in the world couldn't have run enough champagne and port and brandy and good old Jamaica rum past the Union blockade to keep the rebel gentry properly lubricated (not that they imbibed any more than their Northern counterparts). Corn whiskey is what they had, and corn whiskey is what they drank.

Still, we can easily picture Old Jube—a man known to tipple, mind you—rudely pushing aside the proffered cup of corn, most likely with a curse. "I was never blessed with popular or captivating manners," he wrote in his memoirs, "and the consequence was that I was often misjudged and thought to be haughty and disdainful in my temperament." Nothing personal, in other words. Matter of principle, and you don't bend on principles. He never did surrender, incidentally—escaped to Mexico instead, dressed up as a 'farmer.'

Did Early himself have anything to do with the formulation of this fine, balanced punch? Our Lawton Mackall, who included it in his December, 1941 "Potables" column, implies that he did, we know not on what evidence. But Mackall came from solid Southern stock, so we're willing to give him the benefit of the doubt. Like the general, anyway, the punch is tart and strong, although a tad sweeter than Lee's 'Bad Old Man' was ever known to be. And if this *was* what kept him going, well, we'd still rather have Ulysses S. Grant's whiskey—but that's almost entirely for military reasons.

JUBAL EARLY PUNCH

Recruit:

1 bottle brut champagne

1½ cups brandy

4 oz Jamaica rum

1 quart plus 1 cup water

1 cup lemon juice

1 cup bar sugar

Dissolve the sugar in the lemon juice and water, pour in the hooch, and let stand for half an hour or so in a cool place for interjubilation to occur.

When serving time is at hand, pour in the champagne, load the bowl with a cannonball of ice and charge!

ADMIRAL VERNON'S LIME GROG

In a large bowl or jar, mix 16 oz fresh-squeezed lime juice and 1 lb. of brown sugar (you may want to use less—try starting with ½ lb. and working your way up)

Dilute with ½ gallon water and 16 oz of old-fashioned dark rum—Jamaica, Demerara, Bermuda, like that

Drop in 5 to 6 sprigs of mint

Refrigerate and serve on the rocks (unless you're a stickler for historical accuracy)

This is a so-called 'four water' grog, four parts water to one of rum. You can always tighten it up, although once you're in two-water territory you'll quickly find your guests "stupefying their rational qualities, which makes them heedlessly slaves to every passion," as the good Admiral warned.

(Leave out the rum and use the full pound of brown sugar and you've got a delightful punch for your kid's birthday party. Them what wants can always hit their ration with a 'stick', as it used to be called, of the ol' kill-devil. Just keep the bottle out of range of little hands.)

ADMIRAL VERNON'S LIME GROG

On August 21, 1740, Admiral Edward 'Old Grogram' Vernon of the Royal Navy issued the following Order to Captains:

Whereas it manifestly appears ... to be the unanimous opinion of both Captains and Surgeons, that the pernicious custom of the seamen drinking their allowance of rum in drams, and often at once, is attended with many fatal effects to their morals as well as their health ... and which ... cannot be better remedied than by ordering their half pint of rum to be daily mixed with a quart of water, which they that are good husbandmen may . . . purchase sugar and limes to make more palatable to them.

We've never heard 'husbandman' used to mean 'bartender' before, but there it is—the Rosetta Stone of the rum drink. All is now clear: we don't add lime juice and sugar to rum to make us drink more of it, but rather less of it. As any true pirate knows, good dark rum goes down so easily on its own that it doesn't really need a mixer taking up valuable rum space. Only something really tasty can make us forget that.

It's obvious the Admiral didn't invent this combination; he was too quick out of the gate with it for that. Rum, sugar, lime juice, water were the rock-bottom basics of tropical tippling, then as now. Freeze the water and you've got a **Daiquiri** or a **Planter's Punch**, depending on the size of the ice and the color of the rum. But if you've a mind to "splice the mainbrace," as they say in the Royal Navy, Old Grogram-style ('grogram', by the way, was a kind of heavy, water-resistant cloth that the Admiral used to sport; abbreviated, the word was soon tacked onto the basic rum-and-water combo that he mandated), you should probably use brown sugar—it's doubtful that the ordinary Jack Tar could've laid his mitts on the ultra-refined white stuff.

Mint Julep, Community Style

"A lifesaver for country hosts," our Murdock Pemberton dubbed this one. That was back in July, 1938, in that uneasy time between the development of the germ theory of disease and the adoption of penicillin. But we're willing to trust that Mr. Pemberton knew something about the germ-killing properties of good bourbon, and work our straws undaunted. Besides, we've got Zithromax.

Pisco Punch

From January, 1848, when gold was discovered in the general area, to the great earthquake of April 18, 1906, San Francisco was the most wide-open town in North America, and that includes New Orleans. Whoring, gambling, doping, thieving—both petty and institutional—fighting, kidnapping, slaving, killing and every other unsavory –ing of which an inflamed human appetite might conceive went virtually unchecked, the occasional hangings arranged by vigilante committees of enraged citizens notwithstanding.

Unusually thirsty work, being that bad. American mixology, then in its vigorous early manhood, did not shrink from the challenge of slaking that thirst (indeed, 'Frisco saw Professor Jerry Thomas—see the **Tom and Jerry**—begin his rise, in 1849). You could get a good drink there—unless, of course, you were an able-bodied sailor, in which case you were liable to be served a **Miss Piggott Special** (equal parts whiskey, brandy and gin, laced with opium), knocked on the head and shipped out to Shanghai.

But if there was one drink that pulled 'em in far and wide, it was the world-renowned (literally) Pisco Punch, as served at the Bank Exchange, a bar that long flourished on the spot where the Transamerica pyramid now stands. Pisco, an odd kind of clear South American brandy, had come to town with the Chileans and Peruvians who heard about the gold and thought they'd take a poke. Sometime between 1854, when the joint opened, and the late 1870s, when owners Orrin Dorman and John Torrance sold it to a close-

MINT JULEP, COMMUNITY STYLE

Place about 50 fresh mint sprigs in a crock or pitcher and pour 4 oz water and 4 oz dark Jamaica rum over them

Add ¼ pound of instant-dissolving bar sugar and macerate the leaves thoroughly

Now take your punch bowl, half-full of cracked, crushed, chipped or shaved ice, and place it on a table under a tree or somewhere else appropriately cool

Strain the mint infusion over the ice; do not permit any of the stems or mash to seep through

Next pour on two bottles of best bourbon and garnish with a small forest—what is that, a copse?—of mint sprigs

Finally, stick straws around the edge of the bowl, one for each guest. "At a given signal, tell them to heave to," as Pemberton puts it.

PISCO PUNCH

Take a fresh pineapple. Cut it in squares about ½ by 1½ inches. Put these squares of fresh pineapple in a bowl of gum syrup (see below) to soak overnight. That serves the double purpose of flavoring the gum syrup with the pineapple and soaking the pineapple, both of which are used afterwards in the Pisco Punch.

In the morning, mix the following in a big bowl:

8 oz of the gum syrup, pineapple flavored as above

16 oz distilled water

10 oz lemon juice

1 bottle (24 oz) Peruvian pisco brandy

Serve very cold but be careful not to keep the ice in too long because of dilution. Use 3- or 4-oz punch glasses. Put one of these above squares of pineapple in each glass. Lemon juice or gum syrup may be added to taste.

Note: The secret ingredient here, gum (a.k.a. 'gomme') syrup, is a nineteenth-century bar essential consisting of sugar syrup which has gum arabic (the crystallized sap of the acacia tree) in it to smooth it out and add body. To make it, slowly stir 1 pound gum arabic into 16 oz distilled water and let soak for a day or two. When this solution is ready, bring 4 pounds sugar and 1 quart distilled water to a boil, add the gum solution and skim off the foam. Let it cool, filter it through cheesecloth and bottle it. It should keep, even unrefrigerated. It's worth the hassle. Really. (See Last Call on page 188 on where to find gum arabic.)

mouthed Scottish immigrant by name of Duncan Nicol, somebody mixed some pisco with a few simple ingredients in careful proportion and alchemy occurred (it might've been Torrance; the bar was also known as 'Pisco John's').

The result? A drink which one initiate compared to "the scimitar of Haroun whose edge was so fine that after a slash a man walked on unaware that his head had been severed from his body until his knees gave way and he fell dead to the ground." The recipe was a tightly guarded secret, the drink itself anything but. Every greenhorn, every tourist, had to stop at the Bank Exchange and receive communion. Things went on like that until Prohibition, when Nicol had to close up shop. He died before repeal, and did his best to take the recipe with him. As far as the general drinking public knew, it was lost forever. Yet Nichols' bar manager, one John Lannes, had been a little too foxy for the old man. What's more, Lannes, eventually, spilled the beans. The California Historical Society published the formula in 1973. Here it is verbatim, repetitious diction and all.

REGENT'S PUNCH

The Prince Regent was a pig. George Augustus Frederick, son of the mad George III, was smart like pigs are, but of course that's not what we mean. Prinnie, as his buds called him, had more than his fair share of appetite for the delights of the flesh. Chiefly fucking, to be sure—he could keep any number of 'amusements' going at once—but also eating, and he had no problem with strong drink except when there wasn't enough. As a consequence, there are about one-and-a-half billion different recipes for Regent Punch, each claiming "to have been held in high esteem" by his Nibs. He must've drank punch like George Washington slept or Jackie O. shopped—everywhere.

In his later years, once the Royal Pop had snuffed it and Prinnie became Kingie, he spent his evenings inhaling a certain punch made up by his maître d', one Mr. Maddison. "That was the only time he was agreeable," according to one observer ("there never was an individual less regretted by his fellow-creatures," quoth *The Times* when he died). We've been unable to locate Mr. M's precise recipe, but this little Regency speedball—note the tea—is close enough.

REGENT'S PUNCH

16 oz strong- brewed black or green tea

Thin-cut rinds of 4 lemons

12 oz bar sugar

6 oz lemon juice

1½ cups orange juice

1 cup unsweetened pineapple juice

1 pint brandy

16 oz dark Jamaican rum

2 bottles brut champagne

Put the lemon rinds into the tea while the latter is still hot, allowing them to steep together; add the sugar and set aside to cool

When cold, add the fruit juices and the liquor; place in a punch bowl with one or two large chunks of ice, adding the champagne immediately before serving

Garnish with orange and pineapple slices. (If you were to cut the brandy in half, lose the rum and pineapple juice and pitch in a bottle of Madeira, your fellow-creatures would not turn up their snouts.)

WHITE WINE CUP

Mix in punch bowl:

1 bottle white burgundy or dryish Graves

4 oz sherry (amontillado or cream)

2 oz brandy (or 1 oz brandy and 1 oz anisette)

Rind of 1 lemon

Bar sugar in moderation—an ounce or less

Add a brick of ice and 1 liter of chilled club soda

Garnish with thin slices of fresh pineapple and sprigs of mint.

WHITE WINE CUP

There are, we've been told, some social occasions where liquor is simply not appropriate. There's hardly any in this old warm-weather friend.

Use the kind with a cork. ▼

PUNCHES, ARCTIC

EGGNOG

"To tradition-steeped Christmas celebrants, the season would be bleak unless thickly upholstered with Eggnog."—*Handbook for Hosts*, 1949. Since then, every ingredient of this seasonal necessity has been proven to be the nutritional equivalent of sucking on the tailpipe of a crosstown number 7 bus. And together? Raw eggs, refined white sugar, liquor, whole milk and heavy cream—damn!

Yet those 'tradition-steeped celebrants' knew a thing or two about getting through a day of full-family jacket. Rather than watch the frown lines on Aunt Henrietta's face harden as you engulf enough **Highballs** to keep you from sticking your head in the fireplace, why not get richly upholstered under the banner of Norman Rockwellian good cheer and holiday spirit? No frowns, everybody's happy. Sort of.

There are as many versions of Eggnog as there are unhappy families; here's a couple of the most valiant.

RAPPAHANNOCK EGGNOG

1 dozen egg yolks (no whites used at all)

¾ cup bar sugar

3 pints best bourbon

12 oz full-bodied rum with plenty of 'nose' to it

4 oz peach brandy

3 pints milk

1 pint whipped cream

Beat yolks in a kitchen bowl for 30 minutes—an electric mixer is a good reprieve

Add the sugar gradually, with no letup

Shot by shot, add the 3 liquors, followed by the milk

Last of all, the whipped cream; if the latter isn't interpolated until the next day, so much the better.

VIRGINIA EGGNOG

1 dozen eggs (separated)

¾ cup granulated sugar

1 generous pint cognac

1½ pint (on the slim side) full-bodied Jamaican rum

1 pint milk

½ pint heavy cream

Grated nutmeg

Put the egg whites aside for the moment

Beat the yolks strenuously, slowly adding ¾ cup of granulated sugar, continuing at tempo until the sugar is entirely dissolved

Slowly pour in the cognac, still stirring all the while

Follow with the rum (pouring the liquor into the yolks has the effect of cooking them more lovingly than any stove could)

Stir in milk and cream (cream may be whipped, but this makes the result a bit rich for some)

Clean off egg-beating equipment and go at the whites until they stand without hitching

Fold the whites into the mixture

Stir in the grated nutmeg

If the nog is too sweet, splash in a little extra cognac to taste.

HOT TODDY

Scrape 12 sugar cubes against the rinds of 2 lemons, infusing them with lemon oil. Squeeze the lemons and combine the juice in a punch bowl with the sugar cubes and 1 quart rye, bourbon, Scotch, Irish or Canadian whiskey (or applejack, or brandy, or Jamaica rum)

Dilute with 2 quarts boiling water (or as per own judgment)

Add a couple of sticks of cinnamon, broken up into pieces

Stir and serve steaming hot with a clove-studded lemon slice in each drink.

Note: For an individual portion, muddle a lemon-rubbed sugar cube in a generous shot of your favorite hooch, toss in a bit of broken-up cinnamon stick and top off with boiling water to taste. Float a clove-studded lemon slice on top.

HOT TODDY

Before the days of reliable central heating, chemistry had to supply what thermodynamics couldn't. Folks drank this sort of thing every day. We don't recommend that. But every once in a while, it's almost worth turning the furnace off and having your own little Victorian house. Just turn it back on before you get to laundry day.

▼ To hell with physics—thermal energy *can* be created.

JAMAICAN HOT TEA PUNCH

What they need with a hot punch in Jamaica—average temperature: 82° F (28° C)—we'll never know. Our Lawton Mackall, when he presented this one back in 1942, provided no explanation. But if the name of this suave and pleasant decoction isn't merely due to its dominant ingredient, then we'll have to assume that somewhere up in the Blue Mountains there's a hollow so sheltered from the balmy breezes which caress the island that its denizens are forced, on occasion, to resort to liquids such as this to maintain their 98.6.

Whatever its origins, this is one of the few hot punches that are entirely free from Christmas spices, which—as we've observed elsewhere (see the **Sensation**)—have been known to cloy. If you simmer it, it has the additional advantage of being quite potent early on, when you most need medication, and then—as the alcohol boils off—growing progressively milder, thus preventing you spoiling a perfectly tolerable Xmas by choking the living shit out of your sister's husband for that well-meant but nonetheless incredibly assholish remark about your wife's 'jubblies.' Those summer punches which you cool with a large cake of ice work the same way, which is good—he'll be back over on July 4th.

JAMAICAN HOT TEA PUNCH

Mix in a large metal pot on the stove or in front of the Yule fireplace:

1 pint dark Jamaican rum

1 pint decent brandy

2 oranges, sliced into thin wheels

1 lemon (or lime), similarly sliced

3 pints hot black tea, freshly brewed

Sugar to taste—at least 1 tablespoon

Pour into mugs, the more rustic the better. If using the stove method, keep this at the lowest simmer you can manage; if the fireplace method, mull by plunging a red-hot poker into each. "Makes six generous drinks"—so says our 1949 *Handbook for Hosts*, anyway. That works out to 5⅓ ounces of hooch per. Just so you know.

NEGUS

Pare off the yellow rind of one lemon in thin strips

Put it into a double boiler with juice of the same, 2 tablespoons of sugar, and 1 bottle of ruby port

Heat, stirring until the sugar is dissolved

When hot, add 1 cup boiling water and strain into a preheated pitcher

Pour into glasses or cups, with or without a flick of nutmeg. Serves a dozen light drinkers or four Anglo-Saxons.

NEGUS

Ancient, ancient, ancient. Colonel Francis Negus was an expert in heraldry (he was once secretary to the Duke of Norfolk, who was in charge of that sort of thing). This fact has no apparent bearing on the mild and very pleasant drink that carries his name, which he is said to have invented during the reign of either Queen Anne (1702–1714) or George I (1714–1727). In any case, the Colonel had to have invented it before 1732, because that's when he died (at a ripe old age, we're pleased to note).

TOM AND JERRY

Supposedly invented in the early 1850s by 'Professor' Jerry Thomas—the Bolivar of American drinking—at the Planters' House hotel, St. Louis, the Tom and Jerry was a holiday favorite for a century. Before Prohibition, every saloon worth wrecking with a hatchet kept a bowl of the batter on the bar from roughly November to March (generally not the *same* bowl, although some of those joints…). After that, it was mostly made at home, until the 1960s, with their thirst for novelty and mania for convenience, killed it off. But you can still find the mugs—little white ceramic things with "Tom & Jerry" printed in gold—in back-country thrift shops (or on eBay, of course).

TOM AND JERRY

Separate a dozen eggs. Beat up the whites until they form a stiff froth, and the yolks—to which you have added ½ pound bar sugar—"until they are as thin as water," as the Professor advises, gradually adding 4 oz brandy (spiceaholics will also add a pinch each of ground allspice, cinnamon and cloves)

Fold the whites into the yolks

When ready to serve, give it another stir and then put 1 tablespoon of this batter in a small mug or tumbler

Now add 1 oz of brandy (although some die-hard Dixiecrats prefer bourbon) and 1 oz of Jamaica rum, stirring constantly to avoid curdling

Fill to the top with hot milk and stir until you get foam

Sprinkle a little grated nutmeg on top. This one may require practice and a certain amount of fiddling, but it's well worth the effort.

Note: Some, finding the milk too rich and filling, use half hot milk, half boiling water.

Last night I tumbled off the water cart—
    It was a peacherino of a drunk;
    I put the cocktail market on the punk
And tore up all the sidewalks from the start.

The package that I carried was a tart
    That beat Vesuvius out for sizz and spunk,
    And when they put me in my little bunk
You couldn't tell my jag and me apart.

Oh! would I were the ice man for a space,
    Then might I cool this red-hot cocoanut,
    Corral the jim-jam bugs that madly race
Around the eaves that from my forehead jut—
    Or will a carpenter please come instead
    And build a picket fence around my head?

—FROM *THE LOVE SONNETS OF A HOODLUM*, BY WALLACE IRWIN (1901)

THE OVERHANG

"THERE IS NO CURE FOR THE HANGOVER," as Robert Benchley said, "save death." All you can really do is drink lots of water and remember not to hate yourself in the morning (a trick we've never quite succeeded in pulling off).

And if you've got a favorite folk remedy, that can't hurt either—it's always better to live in hope than despair. We don't recommend the hair-of-the-dog routine—personally, we don't even want to look at the stuff. But lots of people do things we don't recommend, us included, and the old 'corpse reviver' has a long and fertile tradition. (We always think of jazzman Eddie Condon's version: "Take the juice of two bottles of whiskey…." *Rimshot*.). Which is to say, here are a few tried-and-trues.

BLOODY MARY

This "savage combination of tomato juice and vodka"—as master bartender Jack Townsend deemed it half a century ago—has managed, in the fullness of time, to escape the "Freak Drink" category where he located it. Like the proverbial pushcart-vendor's kid, the Bloody Mary went from the Lower East Side to Scarsdale in one generation, shedding along the way its queer foreign ways for one of pure, Anglo lineage.

The Bloody Mary's pedigree is, according to the standards we've been operating by in this book, solid: it was invented by Fernand 'the Frog' Petiot in 1921. As the nickname (acquired once he came to America) suggests, Petiot was French. His drink was one of the earliest to use this mysterious vodka stuff that was turning up all over Paris in the company of the uncommunist Russian refugees who had gone to ground there in great numbers. By the mid-1920s, he was working at Harry's New York Bar (see the **White Lady**). Slowly the drink caught on among the international barflies who made Harry's their H.Q.

In 1933, the Frog got restless and hopped over to New York, where he got a job at the King Cole Bar in the St. Regis Hotel. Problem one: no vodka in America. Problem two: the St. Regis was a stuffy, swank sort of joint, and they didn't go for the name Bloody Mary; too vulgar. Enter the **Red Snapper**, which was nothing more than a gin—gak!—Bloody Mary (Petiot switched back to vodka as soon as he could). But the true drink lived on at Harry's, whence apostles like the ever-thirsty, ever-overhung Hemingway spread it throughout the world. Before too long, by dint of constant interaction with the rich and Anglo-Saxonish, all traces of foreignness were rubbed off. In fact, this upstart is now second only to the **Martini** in the world of WASP drinking.

Whatever its current status, a glance at the Bloody Mary's component parts—neutral spirits, restorative juices, salts, capsaicins and other volatile oils—indicates that its origins lie in the shadowy world of the hangover cure, and there, as far as we (snobbish to the core in these matters) are concerned, it may remain, a useful citizen of the Republic of Tipple, but never to be enrolled in the Social 400.

BLOODY MARY

Shake well with cracked ice:

2 oz vodka

4 oz tomato juice

½ tablespoon lemon juice

Generous splash Worcestershire sauce

3 to 4 dashes Tabasco sauce

1 teaspoon fresh grated horse-radish, with the liquid squeezed out

Strain into Collins glass with 2 or 3 ice cubes in it

Add a pinch of salt and fresh-ground pepper, to taste.

Garnish, if necessary, with stalk of celery (a Chicago innovation, that).

CHAMPAGNE

'Tis an expensive restorative, no doubt; but, just as you cannot make an omelette without breaking eggs, so are most of our pleasant vices more or less costly in the long run. Champagne, i.e. genuine champagne, is about the most valuable restorative known to science.

—EDWARD SPENCER MOTT, 1899

For especially virulent cases, some textbooks prescribe the addition of ½ oz brandy and ½ teaspoon Grand Marnier to the straight fizzy. This treatment is known as the **Barbotage**, French for 'bubbling'.

COCA-COLA

For our money, the sovereign non-alcoholic hangover cure remains a 20-oz Coca-Cola (*not* Diet Coke) absorbed straight from the bottle. For those unfamiliar with this sweet brown concoction, it's a carbonated patent tonic with a certain amount of caffeine that occasionally turns up in the **Cuba Libre**.

◀ **Sometimes you spring right back (and sometimes you don't).**

EYE-OPENER

We recall hearing somewhere that to convey his morning drink to his mouth without shaking it all out of the glass, Eugene O'Neill would bum a towel from the bartender (he was known to the establishment), drape it around his neck, take an end in each hand, and pull it taut. He would then use one hand to pull the other—and the shot of whiskey in it—to his mouth, the tension of the towel damping the shakes.

If that's what it takes to get you going in the morning, you're not gonna need to be messing around with orange curaçao and apricot brandy, let alone grenadine and egg yolks. The straight creature is what you want. But if it's just a case of over-celebrating the successful completion of the Big Project, something like that, then this little so-and-so from *Esquire*'s 1949 *Handbook for Hosts* might just be the thing to turn that frown upside down (provided you're okay with morning drinking; we go both ways). It's sweet and strong, anyway, and the egg yolk gives it *some* nutritive value.

EYE-OPENER

Shake strenuously with cracked ice (the cracking and shaking should provide a good proportion of the exercise that smug bastards of the medical variety prescribe for your condition):

2 oz old Haitian rum (basically, Barbancourt)

½ teaspoon orange curaçao

½ teaspoon apricot brandy

1 teaspoon grenadine

1 egg yolk

Strain into chilled cocktail glass (or Old-Fashioned glass, which is easier to hold, even without the towel).

MORNING AFTER

Shake violently with cracked ice (see the **Eye-Opener**):

2 oz absinthe (if you use home-made, repeat: "What doesn't kill me makes me stronger")

1 teaspoon anisette (even sambucca will do)

1 egg white

Strain into Old-Fashioned glass and splash in a little club soda or seltzer on top.

PRAIRIE OYSTER

Crack an egg into an Old-Fashioned glass, leaving the yolk unbroken

Dose it with 1 teaspoon Worcestershire sauce, a sprinkling of salt and pepper, and a couple of dashes Tabasco sauce

Down at a gulp.

MORNING AFTER

If you've got plenty of absinthe around, and your over-hang is of the Stalingrad variety, this might do the trick: absinthe is a pretty good stomach-tonic, and the 120 proof doesn't hurt, either.

PRAIRIE OYSTER

This one was formerly quite popular, until the drinking public became unfamiliar with the use of the raw egg. Supposedly full of nutrients, with a hit of pepper to kickstart the stomach.

SEA CAPTAIN'S SPECIAL

Credited to Seattle bartender Harry Porter, whose clientele had a nautical cast, this "distilled dynamite"—as we labeled it back in 1949—represents traditional mixology's most concerted effort towards cleaning up the mess that follows the injudicious use of its products.

Like any monumental edifice, it starts with a sound foundation: in this case, an **Old-Fashioned** (whose eponymous glass, we should note, is graspable by all but the shakiest of hands). To this, Porter added an upper story of champagne—the bubbles speed up the delivery of the ol' C_2H_5OH—and a frieze of absinthe, for the stomach (any herbalist will tell you, wormwood is particularly soothing to that much-abused organ).

We have tested the S.C.S.'s efficacy. The circumstances are neither important nor unaccompanied by embarrassment. It works, insofar as any cure based on the principle of *pilus canis mordentis*—'hair of the dog', in the vulgate—can be said to work. You will not be so hung over today, but tomorrow… Unless, of course, you just keep drinking. But we don't advise that, do we? Which is why we reserve Harry Porter's magic potion only for those rare, horrifying occasions when chemistry (see **Coca-Cola**) has already failed us.

SEA CAPTAIN'S SPECIAL

In an Old-Fashioned glass, place a sugar cube (or ½ teaspoon loose sugar)

Wet this down with 2 or 3 dashes of Angostura bitters and a short splash of water or club soda

Crush the sugar with a muddler or whatever's handy

Rotate the glass so that sugar grains and bitters give it a lining

Add a large ice cube

Pour in 2½ oz rye or bourbon

Top off with brut champagne and 2 dashes absinthe (if you lack this ingredient, you may use one of the substitutes available—Absente, Herbsaint, Pernod, etc.—but since they contain no wormwood, their effect will be, let's say, psychosomatic).

SUFFERIN' BASTARD

Shake well with cracked ice:

1 oz bourbon

1 oz London dry gin

1 teaspoon lime juice

Dash Angostura bitters

Strain into Collins glass with 2 or 3 ice cubes, top up with ginger ale and gently slip in 2 sprigs of mint.

Before and after? Not quite, but Egypt's contribution to mixology is still a fine drink. ▼

SUFFERIN' BASTARD

Shepheard's Hotel, 8 Shari'a Kâmil, Cairo: 350 rooms, 150 with bath (in 1929, anyway), garden, terrace, restaurant, grill and—most important—bar. It was one of those places, like the Hotel Nacional in Havana (see the **Hotel Nacional Special**) or the Raffles in Singapore (see the **Singapore Sling**) where the people who run things for the rest of us crossed paths, a miniature republic of its own peopled by the powerful, the restless, the bored, the curious, the rich.

In the 1940s, the man behind the Long Bar at Shepheard's was a guy named Joe Scialom. He'd been a bar steward—that's Brit for bartender—all over the world, including Brooklyn, but Cairo granted him immortality. It was there, you see, he found himself "searching desperately for a pickup after a bad night," as *Esquire* reported in 1947. His solution—originally known as the 'Suffering Bar Steward', a title easily misheard by the afflicted—goes straight to the root of the problem. You are hung over when you are no longer drunk; therefore, to be un-hung, you must be re-drunk. And the SB(S) is as pleasant a way of redrinking as any we know—so pleasant, in fact, it's almost worth having that extra tray of jello shots the night before just so you can have one of these the morning after.

Shepheard's burned down during anti-British rioting in 1952, but its bar steward lives on.

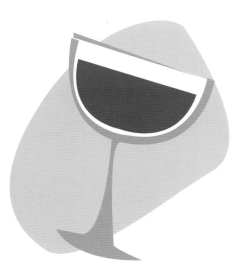

SOME BRANDS

We mixed an awful lot of drinks while preparing this book, and we thought it would be a friendly gesture to let you know some of the brands of hooch we used, if only to give you somewhere to start when you're in the liquor store. These are by no means the only good brands out there—in fact, they're not even the best ones, from a sipping point of view. There's no point in wasting super-premium liquor in mixed drinks. Neither, though, should you mix drinks with liquor you wouldn't drink straight (certain liqueurs excepted). This is all good, cocktail-grade liquor, and will generally set you back well under $30 a bottle.

BRANDY/COGNAC *(generally, the most expensive of the standard liquors)*
> Hennessy, Courvoisier, Martell, Rémy Martin (all VS-grade cognacs); Raynal (brandy)

WHISKY, SCOTCH
> White Horse, Dewar's

WHISKEY, IRISH
> John Power's, Jameson's, Old Bushmills

WHISKEY, STRAIGHT RYE
> Wild Turkey 101, Old Overholt (a.k.a. 'Old Overcoat'), Jim Beam

WHISKEY, BOURBON
> Wild Turkey 101; Old Forester 100–proof, Old Grand-Dad 100–proof

VODKA
> Stolichnaya (red label), Finlandia, Ketel One

GIN
> Bombay Sapphire, Tanqueray, Beefeater

RUM, JAMAICAN-STYLE *(and other styles of the British Caribbean)*
> Myers's, Coruba (Jamaica); Gosling's Black Seal (Bermuda); Lemon Hart 151 (Demerara-style, from Guyana)

RUM, CUBAN-STYLE DARK
> Brugal añejo (Dominican Republic); Ron del Barilito 2-star, Bacardi Select (Puerto Rico)

RUM, CUBAN-STYLE WHITE

    Brugal (Dominican Republic), Fernandes 19 (Trinidad), Bacardi Carta
Blanca (Puerto Rico)

RUM, HAITIAN AND OTHER FRENCH CARIBBEAN *(rhum agricole)*

    Barbancourt 5-star (Haiti); St. James, J. Bally (Martinique)

TEQUILA

    Herradura silver; Sauza Commemorativo

VERMOUTH

    Martini and Rossi (Italian/sweet/red); Noilly Prat (French/dry/white)

SOME MEASUREMENTS

128 oz	**=**	**1 gallon**
32 oz	**=**	**1 quart**
25.6 oz	**=**	**⅘ quart = ⅕ gallon (a fifth)**
16 oz	**=**	**1 pint**
8 oz	**=**	**1 cup**
1 oz	**=**	**2 tablespoons**
¾ oz	**=**	**1½ tablespoons**
⅔ oz	**=**	**1 tablespoon + 1 teaspoon**
½ oz	**=**	**1 tablespoon = 3 teaspoons**
⅓ oz	**=**	**2 teaspoons**
¼ oz	**=**	**½ tablespoon = 1½ teaspoons**
⅙ oz	**=**	**1 teaspoon**
⅛ oz	**=**	**¼ tablespoon**
1/12 oz	**=**	**½ teaspoon = 1 splash**
1 dash	**=**	**¼ splash, more or less**

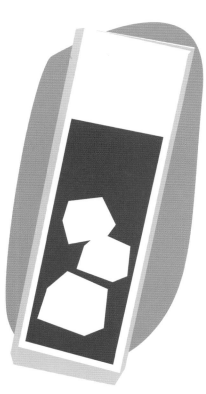

BIBLIOGRAPHICAL NOTE

Our library here at the Esquire Institute is extensive (although not as extensive as some—Budget Department take note). However, out of the hundred-odd drink books we've consulted during the preparation of the current volume, there are only a few we can recommend without reservation. *Esquire*'s own books, of course—*Esquire's Liquor Intelligencer*, 1939 (well, we've never actually seen a copy of this one; if anyone out there has it…). *Esquire's Handbook for Hosts*, 1949. *Esquire Drink Book*, 1956. *Esquire's Party Book*, 1965. *Esquire's [new] Handbook for Hosts*, 1973. *Esquire's Wine and Liquor Handbook*, 1984. Of these, the most authoritative is the comprehensive and amusing 1956 *Drink Book*. We bow to Frederic A. Birmingham, its editor (even if he was known to be partial to the **Brandy Alexander**).

Our pick for best bar book of all time, however, is Albert Stevens Crockett's 1931 *Old Waldorf Bar Days* (re-edited four years later as *The Old Waldorf-Astoria Bar Book*, which was reprinted in 1998; seek it out). Among the other old classics, we've derived particular benefit from David Embury's 1948 *Fine Art of Mixing Drinks* (the only theoretical work on mixology), Jack Townsend and Tom Moore McBride's no-bullshit *Bartender's Book* (1951), and George J. Kappeler's 1895 *Modern American Drinks*. Among the moderns, *Straight Up or On the Rocks*, William Grimes' witty and skeptical cocktail history, is indispensable, as are Lowell Edmunds' work on the Martini, Jim Murray's on whisk(e)y in general and Gary Regan and Mardee Haidin Regan's on bourbon in specific.

LAST CALL *(Sources for a few hard-to-find items)*

LIQUORS AND LIQUEURS Your local liquor store (if it's not the kind with armored glass) can order just about anything in this book. Or you can try Costa Mesa, California's Hi-Time Wine Cellars, perhaps the best liquor store in America: (800) 331-3005; www.hitimewine.com. They'll ship to wherever it's legal. **FEE BROTHERS' WEST INDIAN ORANGE BITTERS** Fee Brothers, 456 Portland Avenue, Rochester NY 14605; (716) 544-9530. **PEYCHAUD'S BITTERS** The Sazerac Co.: (504) 831-9450; www.sazerac.com/bitters.html. **ORANGE FLOWER WATER** Mymouné, our favorite brand, is sometimes available from Sahadi Imports, 187 Atlantic Avenue, Brooklyn, NY 11201; (718) 439-7779. **GUM ARABIC** Frontier Co-op carries this in a handy powder; www.frontiercoop.com. Wherever you get it from, make sure it's food-grade.

DRINKS INDEX

RULE #1

When all else
fails, have a
Martini.

INGREDIENTS INDEX